The Mother-Son Running Streak Club

How I bonded with my nine-year-old son
by running a mile with him every day for a year

A memoir

by

Nancy Shohet West

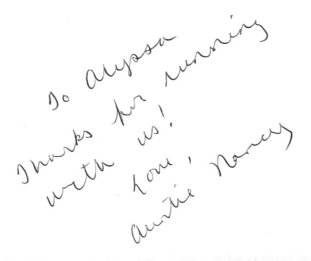

Articles were reprinted with permission from
the *Boston Globe* and the *Carlisle Mosquito*.

In a few cases, names have been changed.

ISBN 1453857052

To Rick and Holly,

for always waiting patiently when we headed out the door

and greeting us lovingly when we returned

INTRODUCTION

Between August 15th of 2007 and August 15th of 2008, the four members of my immediate family each turned a year older: forty-one for me, forty for my husband Rick, nine for Tim and six for Holly. The war in Iraq reached its fifth anniversary and racked up a total of four thousand casualties. Benazir Bhutto, prime minister of Pakistan, was assassinated. The Boston Red Sox won their second 21st-century World Series championship. In an unprecedented presidential campaign season that focused on issues ranging from health care to illegal immigration to how to fix the mortgage crisis, a female senator and an African-American senator made history as they faced off against each other long past the point where the race has usually narrowed to one finalist per party. The summer Olympic Games began in Beijing.

And my son Tim and I ran at least one mile every single one of those 366 days. (It was a Leap Year.)

Here's how. And why.

CHAPTER 1

August 12 – September 11, 2007

By the last third of the summer of 2007, my exasperation, like the August heat and New England humidity, had risen to a crest. I was weary of gazing into my eight-year-old son's pallid face and wondering what it would take to make this child happy.

Like other mothers, I look at my two children – Tim, who was nearly nine, and his sister Holly, who that summer turned five – and see them surrounded by all the riches one childhood could possibly contain. Not just the basics – clean drinking water, nutritious food, the love of parents and grandparents and aunts and uncles, antibiotics when they are sick and safe open spaces in which to play – and not even just the affluence of any middle-class American child growing up in the suburbs in the first decade of the new millennium. Not even just all the infrastructure that comes with living in the richest, most powerful nation in the world.

My children, it seems to me, have even more. They live in a two-parent household in an unusually close-knit community of five thousand, a town twenty miles west of Boston in which newcomers marvel at the friendliness of neighbors who bring over fresh-baked pies and attendants at the dump who help women lift heavy trash barrels. Even our living situation is uniquely conducive to a happy childhood: we live on four acres carved out of the east end of my parents' farm, a small family-run operation on which we raise organic beef. My kids have a hayloft in which to

1

play, a pond on which to paddle, and two affectionate grandparents living next door.

So in short, my two children are growing up in what seems to me like paradise. And yet despite baseball camp, weekend bike rides and a wonderful family vacation in Colorado, my much-loved eight-year-old son seemed to have hit a downward slump in his emotional well-being that summer.

I had him tested for anemia, but the pediatrician saw nothing wrong. And it's not like this was new. It was just the lowest point of a continuum that I had watched him travel along for his whole young life.

"So he's not gregarious," his second-grade teacher had said at our last conference of the past school year, brushing off my concerns.

"He's a thinker, an introvert," said his kindergarten teacher two years earlier.

I'm his mother, and of course I love him, and I love so many things *about* him: his generally serious bearing with occasional sparks of humor or even silliness; his intellect; his devotion to a few specific things (frogs of all kinds, Rick, Holly at certain times but not others).

But he has other traits that are very hard for me to cope with. I often lament that if he's not playing either baseball or video games, he broods. Other than team sports, which he loves, he doesn't like to join afterschool groups. No Scouts, no chess club, no theater class: none of the extracurriculars his friends gravitate toward interest him.

However, how he chooses to spend his time concerns me less than how he seems to feel about other people. I put a high priority on reaching out and making friends; much as I love my husband, I get lonely if I don't have a steady stream of social contact. Holly, as she finishes her preschool years, is like me: she finds people to be interesting and likeable, whether they are children or adults. If I invite a family new to town over for a cookout, Holly's attitude tends to be "You're a kid under the age of ten? Great, let's go find something to do!" Whereas Tim's could be summed up more along the lines of "I probably won't like you much, and also don't touch my baseball cards."

It's not as if I don't know other parents who struggle to get along better with their children, or to correct what they perceive as negative behavioral trends. Plenty of mothers in my circle have consulted with the school guidance counselor, some even with external specialists in childhood issues. Some parents pursue special diets to change their children's moods, or sign them up for more activities. Nearly all the parents I know – myself included – devour books on parenting. We are well-educated professionals; we know how to do our research. We study our kids as if we are earning a dissertation on them rather than raising them.

But as far as I was concerned, it wasn't working very well. Despite my inherent maternal love for Tim, I was tired of playing Tigger to his Eeyore.

So I put aside all the books and theories and tried something different. Something no other parent I knew had done. I didn't buy him hours of therapy or prescription anti-depressants, though sometimes I still think maybe I should have.

I bought him a pair of running shoes.

I'm a freelance journalist. Primarily, I write features for the *Boston Globe*. As a freelancer, I'm generally responsible for finding my own story ideas. So I travel through my day with my ears open for interesting people doing unusual things.

In mid-2005, I discovered something about a man who lives in my town. I knew he was a distance runner; I'd seen him out training on the road many times, and our local newspaper – quaintly named the *Carlisle Mosquito* – posted his finish times for the Boston Marathon every year. But I did not know he was part of an odd and eclectic little group of athletes called *streak runners*.

Streak runners, who have to endure constant jokes about whether they run with their clothes off – which they do not; those are *streakers*, this is different – are runners who have challenged themselves to run at least a mile a day, 365 days a year, without missing a day, for as long as they can. The man in my town, Ronald Kmiec, came to my attention because he was approaching his thirtieth anniversary of streak running. Not since late November of 1975 – the era of the Ford administration and the year that Microsoft was founded – had Kmiec missed a day of running.

But even more astonishing than that was the fact that thirty years doesn't even give him the longest running streak in the U.S. Not even close. Though he's the number-one streak runner in Massachusetts, according to the official registry of the United States Running Streak Association, he's only number thirteen nationwide. The man with the longest streak in the U.S. was approaching *forty* years at the time I decided to write an article on Kmiec for the *Boston Globe*.

To put myself in context as a runner, I have never done a marathon or even a half-marathon. My average time is a ten-minute mile, which if you're an adult between the ages of twenty-five and fifty and in decent shape but have never before laced on a pair of running shoes is probably about what you'd run. In other words, I'm not much of a powerhouse. I'm a plodder.

Yet I've loved running ever since the summer after my freshman year in college, which was the first time in my life I started exercising regularly. And one reason I love it is that it doesn't *matter* that I'm not very good at it. I've often said that to be a long-distance runner, all you really need to do is show up, kind of like Woody Allen said about life.

Of course, that's not precisely true. If you want to be a high-scoring competitive runner, you need speed and muscles. But to *call* yourself a runner, you just need to get out there and run. And that I can do. That I've been doing for years. I'm a mid-distance runner, typically doing three to five miles per workout, and I'm a frequent runner, getting out there four or five times a week, three seasons a year.

I've never liked cold-weather running; when the mercury dips below forty, I turn to my stationary bike for the New England winter. But come the first mild day in March, when the snow banks start shedding rivulets of water into the roadway, my body craves the feeling of pavement pounding in measured rhythm beneath my sneakers, and I'm back out on the road.

Even though I'm no marathoner, from the first time I heard about streak runners, I wondered if it was something I could do. Go running every day? What a great challenge. I happen to be an adult with an inordinate attraction to routine. I love the measured pace of a life in which days are marked by diurnal rituals. I write in my journal no less than one thousand words a day. I go outside just before bed every night to look at the stars and thank the universe for yet another day well passed.

The idea of seeing how long I could sustain a daily running streak intrigued me. And yet I'm also a mother of young children, and we mothers have an innate sense of obligation that causes us to put aside our own inclinations for the good of the family. So slipping out for a daily mile seemed really impractical.

I had given up a full-time job as a copywriter for a travel company when Holly was born. Tim was almost four then. With my freelance journalism career gradually taking shape in the form of a fairly steady flow of writing assignments for the *Boston Globe* and a few other publications, the schedule enabled me to spend the next four years as a stay-at-home mom. I joined the playgroup circuit and went to story times with Holly. I volunteered for as many classroom activities as possible once Tim started kindergarten.

But the realities of our household economics necessitated my return to work in late spring of 2006. My husband, a self-employed financial market analyst, had hit something of a dry spell after several fairly successful years and was struggling with his consulting business. My freelancing didn't bring in enough to support a family of four.

Our mortgage was sky-high and our property taxes were hair-raising, but we had made the choice five years earlier to build a magnificent custom-designed house on the edge of my parents' farm, and selling the house would mean disappointment and potentially family discord all around. It wasn't just a matter of letting down my parents, who gave us the land, but also my sisters, who both live out of state. Knowing we were next door to my parents keeping an eye on them allowed the rest of the family to worry less.

So when I had the chance to accept a full-time position as a corporate communications writer at a biosciences company in a nearby suburb, I felt fortunate, but the transition had presented challenges to all of us. I found it nearly impossible to maintain the household up to my standards while being away from home ten hours a day; the kids, though cooperative about the new childcare schedule, tended to want a lot of proximity to me once I was home, to make up for lost time. Arriving home at the end of the workday only to change into running clothes and head out again would have gone over poorly with the gang, to say the least. Regular running seemed to be just one more casualty of returning to work. I felt lucky to get out occasionally for a run on a late Saturday afternoon, or before church on Sunday.

But in early August of 2007, as I pondered my son's malaise, a new idea came to me.

He had never shown any interest in going running with me. But he's a good athlete – a natural baseball player, decent at soccer and an enthusiast of any kind of pick-up playground game, from touch football to foursquare – and he has a competitive nature when it comes to sports. Had I asked him if he wanted to go running once in a while, he probably would have said no.

But I posed it as a challenge: Want to try to run a mile every day and see how many days we can keep it up?

A challenge. That's what caught his imagination, and I could see that he was turning it over in his mind. "Every day?" he asked.

"Like the man I wrote the article about. We won't do thirty years, like he did. We'll just see what we can do. We'll try to do a week. Or ten days."

"I'll try it," he said with a nonchalant shrug.

"Think you can do a mile?" I asked him.

Another shrug.

"Want to start today?"

He looked momentarily anxious. "How about…Sunday?"

Sunday. Five days away. Five days to build up the anticipation, to get him fired up for the challenge. I was game.

And to my moderate amazement, so was he.

Tim's running log: Sun 8/12, 6 PM. Day 1. 1.5 miles. A little running, a lot of walking. Hard!

Though we had discussed it with mounting anticipation all weekend, I ended up frustrated by our first day of running. I never stopped to consider whether Tim would be able to run one mile nonstop; somehow I just took it on faith that this part of the plan would succeed.

I thought the challenge would be getting him to do it every day, not getting him to do it at all. But two minutes out the front door, he was already walking.

"It's a *run*, Tim!" I called as I passed him at a slow easy jog. "You have to try to *run!*" He ran a little more, then walked again. And that's how the whole thirty minutes passed: I jogged as slowly as I possibly could; Tim walked two minutes for every one he ran.

I tried to tell myself that hearing me shriek like a harridan would in no way make him want to become a better runner. In fact, it would probably be a deterrent to his interest in maintaining this streak plan. But I was irritated by what was going on, and toward the end of the run I realized why. Polite and good-natured as he is toward other people, he has an ability to dig his heels in when he wants to, and it often seems to me that his stubbornness sometimes functions in direct correlation to how important something is to me. I couldn't help but take it as a personal insult that he wasn't trying harder on this run.

Finally, in the last five minutes of the route, a calmer and more rational mood overtook me. I noticed that Tim was continuing to alternate jogging with walking at the end of the run just as he had at the beginning, which I knew was preferable to all running at the beginning and all walking at the end. He deserved credit for rationing his energy and maintaining the same, albeit slow, pace from beginning to end.

Moreover, as hard as it was for me to recall after twenty-two years of running, this is how I started out too: alternating between walking and running. That's how beginners build themselves up.

So despite my frustration, Tim was off to a fine start, and it was beginning to dawn on me that maybe I was the one who had the most to learn from this experiment.

As a journalist, I like people to tell me detailed accounts, and I like to write long stories. At the same time, I always have my ears cocked for the sound bite – the perfect little quote that will begin or end the story and sum up its essence in one or two pithy, unforgettable sentences.

For example, in October of 2006, I covered a local Chinese adoption society's celebration of the Autumn Moon Festival. At the end of this annual tradition, each child launches a paper-cup boat into the water and makes a wish. As one ten-year-old launched her boat, she said to me, "Every year at the Autumn Moon Festival, I wish I could someday meet my birth parents in China, *and* I wish for peppermint stick ice cream. And every year when I open the freezer the next morning, I find peppermint stick ice cream."

It's what I call the rock-star quote. It was the perfect conclusion to my article, and reader response was fantastic. Everyone loved the story – and most of all, everyone loved the quote about peppermint stick ice cream.

There are two sound bites that come to mind when I think about my relationship with Tim. One is something a close friend said about her sister-in-law, who has a lot of trouble getting along with her own son. "Those two are like oil and water," she said.

Tim was just a baby at the time, and the boy in question was about eleven, but her words disturbed me. Is it really possible to be as different from your own child as two fundamentally non-combinable substances like oil and water?

The other sound bite is a story my cousin's wife told me. When her son was eighteen months old or so, she took him to visit her mother-in-law. At some point during their trip, her mother-in-law was having a hectic day and she wanted to get out of the way, so even though she knew it wouldn't be easy to take a toddler to a restaurant alone, she took her son to a local diner and sat him in a high chair opposite her. And she remembers looking at him across the table and thinking, "I think I'm going to like getting to know you."

There have been times throughout Tim's lifetime when I've looked at him and thought, "I think I'm going to like getting to know you." I remember when he was just three or four days old. He had been dozing frequently, the way newborns do, and I was lying in bed next to him. When he woke up, I propped him against my knees so that we were eye level. His round gray-blue eyes – soon to turn dark brown – stared at me and I stared back. We were drinking each other in with our eyes, as if saying "Ah, you're the person I'm going to be getting to know over the next few days. Months. Years. And it's going to be a good process!"

So. The two sound bites, the two extremes. "Oil and water," or "I think I'm going to like getting to know you." The two phrases seem to be opposites; and yet in my experience with Tim, both are entirely true.

Tim's running log: Mon 8/13, 6:30 PM. Day 2. 1.8 miles. A little running, mostly walking. Still hard! Alyssa is sleeping over so she came with us.

By the second day, it seemed we were making tiny steps of progress. My thirteen-year-old niece Alyssa, who is Rick's sister's daughter, had come to visit for a couple of days. She joined us, which made Tim try harder. He did a little more running than he had the day before, though it still seemed to me like mostly walking. I was more patient. I reminded myself to keep my eye on the big picture and remember my goals for this experiment.

I wrote down my goals that first week:

- To improve my relationship with Tim by spending more time together
- To channel Tim's innate love of competition into something that I see as far more honorable than, say, video hockey
- To introduce Tim to the joy of running: the physical exhilaration; the glory of being outside and absorbing the wonders of our surroundings; discovering what our bodies can do
- To embark on something that Tim and I will both find challenging, in the hopes that by doing it together, we'll forge a bond
- To improve our fitness and energy levels

I reminded myself that I wasn't really expecting our first streak attempt, or in fact any streak attempt, to last for 365 days. The goal was just to challenge ourselves. If the first one lasted for three days before we missed a day, then we'd try for four days next.

Tim's running log: Tues 8/14, 6:30 PM. Day 3. 1.8 miles. More running than walking. Felt okay this time.

Compared to most households in town, our location is particularly conducive to running. Although our town is semi-rural, many parts of it are not ideal for walking or biking. Until a year earlier, there were no sidewalks anywhere in town, and the long, winding roads, though scenic, don't leave much room for foot traffic. The thick woods make for poor sight lines, and drivers often aren't expecting to see runners or walkers. It's a particular irony that although we live in a fairly old-fashioned New England community in the country, people on foot or on bikes need to fear for their lives.

For more than a decade, a small grassroots group in town had lobbied for footpaths alongside the major roads. In about 2005, the project finally received funding, and by a happy coincidence, it was on our road that the first footpath was installed. It extended a mile, from the center of town out just past our driveway.

Our house is situated on a common driveway, a long dirt road shared by four households. About three-tenths of a mile off the main road, it splits. Left at the fork takes you to our house first and then to my parents; right at the fork leads to our two other sets of neighbors. From our house, we can run along the common driveway and then onto the footpath along the main road, reaching the town center without ever setting foot in the roadway. Had we lived anywhere else in town, it would have been too dangerous to pledge to run a mile or more every day, especially if we had to go during rush hour or after sunset. But we happened to live along one of the town's only off-road footpaths.

I keep a whiteboard and a set of dry-erase markers on the door that leads from the mudroom into the garage. That's where I record the family's weekly schedule: the kids' activities, Rick's and my evening meetings or social commitments, reminders about who needs to bring a lunch or a permission slip on which days. After our second day of running, I marked a red square at the bottom of the whiteboard in which I penned a bright blue "2" to mark two days of running. Next to it, Tim wrote "Begun August 12."

Watching Tim's long skinny legs flash as he ran filled me with poignant joy. He ran the way kids do – heels kicking up behind, head thrown back. Nothing like the contained and methodical way I run. The first couple of days I tried to explain to him about pacing himself, running slowly in order to run longer, but he didn't seem to understand or want to do that. It didn't matter much to me; I imagined the pacing would evolve on its own eventually.

In those first few days, as we ran together, I felt like I was experiencing Best of Tim: my exuberant, strong, confident boy. For so much of the summer, I'd lived with Worst of Tim: the thin, pale child who burrowed into the arm of the couch with his hands welded to his video game controls. The other side of him typically emerged when he was playing baseball. As my eyes drank in the sight of his flashing limbs running ahead of me on the footpath, I acknowledged that this was why I'd devised this plan: I believed on some level that running would bring Best of Tim out into the light, more and more frequently.

Tim's running log: Wed 8/15, 6:30 PM. Day 4. 1.8 miles. Ran a whole mile, then walked. Felt good.

On our fourth day, Tim completed a continuous mile of running. We were on our usual course into the town center and back, a total of 1.8 miles. After I assured him he'd reached the one-mile mark, which was near his school, he walked most of the way home, breaking into a jog once or twice (and stopping altogether to watch a soccer game for about two minutes as well, insisting he wasn't *resting* but just waiting for me to catch up).

It was dawning on me that there were some ways in which this streak-running program was not a very foresighted idea. For one thing, I was having doubts about convincing Tim of the importance of the streak runner's credo to *never miss a day*. It occurred to me that no matter what the activity, a day off every now and then is almost always a benefit: from school, from piano practice, from the rule of not eating sweets before dinner.

It's the archetypal Sabbath model. Without the promise of a day off to look forward to, I'm not sure anyone can be expected to take on this practice of running. I had said all along that we wouldn't expect to do a 365-day streak from our first time out; we'd start with shorter streaks and build up. Nonetheless, I had to admit that once we broke a streak, there would be little incentive for Tim to start up the next one.

Tim's running log: Thurs 8/16, 6:40 PM. Day 5. 1.6 miles. All running. Felt GREAT.

On Thursday evenings during July and August of that summer, Rick played in an adult softball league. Because he had to leave before I got home from work, he'd take the kids with him, and then I'd meet them up at the softball field after stopping at home to change. When the first Thursday since we began running rolled around, I told Tim before I left for work that he should leave me a note at home as to whether he wanted to go running or not, because if he did, I'd change into running clothes and we could begin our run at the field.

When I got home, there was a white slip of paper on the kitchen counter on which Tim has printed in thick black marker, "Run run run as slow as you can. YES."

I found it very funny that he was teasing me about running slowly. But I changed my clothes and met him up at the field. For the first time, Tim did the whole route at an easy jog, side by side with me. As we ran along, I indulged in the sense that this might have been the happiest moment of my summer so far.

Toward the end, Tim said, "This feels great. I feel like I'm running so well."

Now you get it!, I wanted to cry out. *Now you're a runner!* But I kept my feelings in check, not willing to let my optimism get the best of me.

What I love about running is that it's so non-discriminating. Unlike skiing or tennis or baseball, it requires so little natural talent. I'm a short, rather dumpy person, a terrible athlete in most regards, definitely the storied "last to be picked for every team" in grade school.

But with running, long-distance running at least, you don't have to be naturally talented to be good at it; you just have to get out there and *do* it. I've run in states across the U.S. and countries throughout Europe; on beaches in Venezuela and Aruba; on the top deck of a cruise ship plying the waters of the western Caribbean. I've run when I was pregnant and run when I was postpartum. I've run before dawn in winter and at high noon on the hottest days of the summer.

I depend on it to balance my moods and keep me emotionally centered. And that, ultimately, was why I wanted to introduce Tim to it. Because just maybe, it could be the kind of force on him that it had long been on me.

Tim's running log: Mon 8/20, 6 AM. Day 9. 1.8 miles. All running. Hard work but fun. Nice to be out early in the morning.

From then on, Tim didn't need to alternate running with walking anymore. He was gaining strength and confidence. During our second week of running, we tried going early in the morning, before I left for work, and that worked out well. Not only was Tim eager and energetic; he really appreciated the specialness of being out just after dawn.

At one point, I said to him, "Do you prefer if I run next to you or behind you? I don't want to make you feel like I'm crowding you." And he promptly answered, "Next to." So again, it struck me that maybe what he'd wanted all along was more of me. (More Of Me = an acronym for MOM. Weird.)

As we headed up School Street during our first early-morning run, he said, "I bet I'm the only kid I know who is up right now." Given that it was about six-fifteen rather than, say,

14

four-fifteen, I doubted that was true, but I suggested he might be the only kid he knew who was out *running* just then.

Tim's running log: Tues 8/21, 6 AM. Day 10. 1.8 miles. Cool and sunny.

Hoping to find other parents with insights on what it was like to run with their kids, I went to CoolRunning.com and posted a message on a discussion group devoted to runners:

My 8-year-old son and I are embarking on a "streak running" regime (using the definition of streak-running set by the USRSA). So far we're 9 days in. I'm interested in corresponding with other streak runners as well as other parent/kid running combos.

Over the next couple of days, replies poured in:

I definitely don't advocate an 8-year old running every day. My kids...12, 7, and 6 all run regularly. Typically they run 3-4 days a week and they run a lot of 5K races...some would say too many, but they really enjoy the races. They run with a youth running club that I help coach.

I'm no doctor, but I agree with the previous poster. Not only is the kid growing and it is possible this could have a negative impact on his joints etc, but it is a lot of pressure to put on a kid to have to run everyday regardless of the weather, other commitments, wanting to play with friends, and maybe just not feeling like running one day but feeling pressured to get out there and run.

I agree you shouldn't try to run every day. If your son really wants to do this maybe go for 30 days and then take a day off by celebrating the 31st day.

15

Children should *run every day. If you give kids under 10 years old a wide open place and 3 or 4 kickballs, plenty of free-time and unplug basically everything... they will run.*

I strongly believe one of the best gifts you can give to your kids is the habit of making running--or any other exercises--a daily routine. Don't make it sound like a chore or duty; make it a regular routine. They'll grow up accepting the same routine so much more easily then. I often think of what New Zealand's great Jack Foster said: "I don't train; I just go for a run."

I don't think I would do a streak with an 8 year old. Sorry.

Tim's running log: Thurs 8/23, 6 AM. Day 12. 1.8 miles. Ran slow, I was so tired.

Halfway through our second week of running, I tried to wake Tim early one morning. He shook me off. I sat down next to him on the bed, pulled the blanket off his shoulders, rubbed his back. "Too tired," he muttered. "We'll go after you get home from work."

"We can't today," I reminded him. "Canobie Lake Park, remember?" Tim had been invited to go with a friend to a theme park in southern New Hampshire that evening.

Tim sat up in bed and looked out the window. "Then we won't go," he said. "This can be the end of our first streak." He yawned. "Eleven days is good. We'll start another one soon."

"Okay," I said as neutrally as I could manage. "Are you going back to sleep, then?"

"Yup." He lay down on his side and pulled the covers up to his ear.

"If you change your mind, come get me and we can head out," I said.

He closed his eyes.

I headed downstairs to get the newspaper, mindful of the promise I'd made to myself never to pressure him or to insist we do this. It was his call. It *had* to be his call, or else all the accusers in the on-line forum would be right about what a risky thing I was doing here. He couldn't do it out of pressure from me. He had to do it because he wanted to, and for no other reason.

We'll start again tomorrow, I told myself. *This is just how I expected it to go. A series of short streaks, then maybe eventually a longer one. Eleven days is more than I expected when we started out.*

I was heading into the kitchen when I heard Tim's voice at the top of the stairs. "Mom?"

I looked up. He was standing, barefoot, dressed in his shorts and a t-shirt, hair a rooster's-comb of cowlicks.

"Actually, I do want to go."

Still drowsy, he stumbled down the stairs toward me.

Tim's running log: Fri 8/24, 2:30 PM. Day 13. 1.9 miles. Not that good; hot and uncomfortable.

I was quite surprised by all the negative responses my post attracted on the runners' website. It seemed there were two camps: those who thought I was putting too much pressure on him orthopedically, and those who thought I was putting too much pressure on him emotionally. I expected other runners to wholeheartedly support the plan, especially given the flexibility of my approach. But many seem to find me quite Dickensian.

In a way, though, it's the story of my life. I am, after all, the parent about whom another parent called 911 one mild autumn day when I left my daughter napping in a locked car on a shady side street for ten minutes. I used to let Tim sleep on his tummy when he was an infant, despite the "Back to Sleep" movement popular in his infancy that said infants were safest on their backs – because it was the only way he'd sleep. Ever since Tim was born, I had made decisions that seemed to me rather daring and maybe a little bit questionable but basically a reasonable way to push the envelope – and other parents had been calling me on it, making me feel cavalier and incompetent.

So in an effort to invest my son's rather dissipated energies into a fun and engaging challenge, it was really just the same old thing: I was being viewed as a parent with extremely questionable judgment.

Bummer. I wished someone would say "What a great idea! Hope it works as far as the behavior improvement goes. Let us know!" Nope, no one had said that yet.

Tim's running log: Sat 8/25, 8:30 AM. Day 14. 1.8 miles. Warm day, but sun not high yet. Nice pace. Felt pretty good.

I thought we'd found the perfect running route: first the one-third mile to the main road, then along the footpath into the town center. But two weeks in, Tim asked if we could try a different route.

"I'm tired of seeing the same things every day," he announced.

"Already?" I said. When I was running alone, I would frequently settle on a favorite route and do it day after day for months at a time, until I needed a change of distance or felt like I'd get a better workout if I covered different terrain."I'm surprised," I admitted. "I love looking at the same things every day...and seeing how they change from one day to the next. Every tree, every patch of grass, every cloud pattern."

As I listened to myself talk, I was reminded of the parenting mantra I repeat to myself over and over again because I never seem to learn it: *He's. Not. You.*

Tim's running log: Sun 8/26, 8:15 AM. Day 15. 1.8 miles. No problems. Legs felt loose. Had a good time.

There are certain days when you're a parent that you know you will continually look back on as benchmarks. In late August we had one of those days, when a fairly routine experience seemed to grow increasingly significant and frightening the more I looked back on it.

Tim was scheduled to go to a baseball game with his friend Ryan's family in the evening. At a few minutes after six, I got a phone call from Ryan's mother saying Tim had had a small bike accident, needed us, probably needed stitches. *Well*, I thought at the time, *scrapes and bumps happen to kids, and this is all right.*

And it *was* all right, except the more I thought back on it, the more I came to realize how many phone calls start out that way but become so much worse, and how many moms have evenings like the one I had that night – at home taking care of Holly, waiting for news from Rick who was with Tim in the emergency room – when the stakes are so much higher. I thought of a thirteen-year-old from our town who was in a car accident last year, and imagined her parents waiting to hear whether her injuries were life-threatening and whether she'd ever walk again. And I recalled the awful story of a graduate of my high school who watched her son bike ahead of her straight into a train crossing, where he was struck and killed by a train.

Knowing how unhappy I felt about Tim sailing off a bike and cutting his chin opened my eyes to how horrific it must have been for those parents: reliving the accident, wondering what would happen next. I knew Tim's injuries were minor, but I kept going back to what I'd be worrying about at that moment were circumstances different: how long will the recovery be, am I equipped to deal with a wheelchair, how many nights am I going to spend at the hospital, when will he be able to go back to school, how much will this change his life from here forward.

"Guess that's it for your streak," Rick chuckled when he and Tim returned from the emergency room. "Who would have guessed this was how it would end?"

"It hasn't ended yet," I said quietly to Tim. *No pressure*, I reminded myself. "We'll see how you feel tomorrow."

"Wake me up in the morning like always," he said.

"We can stop any time you want," I said.

19

"No, I'm going to do a 30-year streak," he announced.

The next morning, he was exhausted and wanted to sleep. But at the end of the day, we did a 1.4-mile run up to the soccer fields and back. Our streak remained unbroken.

Tim's running log: Tues 8/28, 6 PM. Day 17. 1.4 miles. Hard because of hills and bike injury, but I was a good sport.

My older sister Lauren and her family arrived the last week in August for a five-day visit. I adore her two daughters and I love having them around. Sophie, who was about to turn fifteen that summer, is smart and fashionable, cheerful yet serene. Phoebe, five years younger, is the kind of person who is forever rallying the group to get a game going and will eventually be every kid's favorite camp counselor. She's big and strong and eminently capable. Needless to say, Tim loves spending time with her because she's so athletic, but she's also a really good example for him because she's so self-reliant and independent. I wished they could be around all the time.

They had spent the previous school year living in a village in France, and Sophie's best friend from France was going to be staying with them for the next several months, so she arrived along with them when they came to visit us in August. Tim was fascinated by her because she was so exotic: not only did she look different from an American teen but she was fluent in another language. Sophie was fairly fluent as well, and even though Tim was too old to let his fascination show, you could tell he was absolutely amazed at the sound of the two of them chattering away together in French.

Tim's running log: Wed 8/29, 6:05 AM. Day 18. 1.8 miles. Nice cool early-morning run. Ribs hurt at first, but then loosened up and felt better.

By the time we'd been running together for three weeks, I realized I'd never expected to make it that far. But something else had not gone the way I expected, either. I was somehow expecting an instant transformation. I was expecting Tim to start running, to *love* running, and to suddenly break out a different personality the way someone might start wearing a new jacket every day.

Not that I actually wanted a different person for my son. But I had thought eighteen days of running would turn him into someone transcendent, someone – well, it was ridiculous to admit, but – someone who would shed all of his eight-year-old-boy idiosyncrasies.

So I was surprised when I took him back-to-school shopping one evening in late August and he was just as twitchy as ever: batting at display racks as we passed them; stubbornly refusing to try on any shirts that had buttons or zippers.

But it was only fair to admit that even if I considered running to be a magical, transformative force in my own life, there were many people who would be quick to argue that it hadn't purged me of all my annoying behaviors either. And Tim would probably be first among them.

Tim's running log: Thurs 8/30, 6:15 AM. Day 19. 1.8 miles. Just about the best day so far. GOOD.

As summer drew to an end, Rick began again talking about selling our house. I love our house and love living on the farm, but even with both of our incomes, it's really difficult for us to make ends meet, and our house is too expensive for us. So this is a discussion that arises every few months.

When I said I did not want to contact the realtor whom we'd talked to off and on for the past year in trying to decide whether to list our house, Rick said, "Your denial is going to drive us into bankruptcy."

I always had so much faith that things would be okay, because as I kept saying to Rick, he would have said the same thing a year ago: we can't possibly make it another year, and yet we had. But he was right that my denial could conceivably drive us into bankruptcy.

It was just a very, very difficult thing for me to face: that we might have to leave the farm, that we might have to admit we'd made a mistake in trying to live there. That ultimately we might have carved up the land my parents gifted us for no good reason, only to abandon it and have someone else, someone we didn't even know, living in the spot my parents had saved for us.

Tim's running log: Fri 8/31, 2:30 PM. Day 20. 1.2 miles. Hot, middle of the day. Not that enjoyable. Sophie went with us.

Tim and I decided to see how many people we could get to go running with us during our streak. We agreed that to qualify, adults had to do a full mile but kids ten and under had to do only a quarter-mile or more. At the end of every month, we could draw up our guest list and see whom we'd gained.

GUEST RUNNERS AND THEIR HOMETOWNS 8/31/07
Sophie R. - Swarthmore, PA
Alyssa A. - Sandwich, MA

Tim's running log: Sat 9/1, 4:30 PM. Day 21. 1.2 miles. With Austin. Big hills but fun anyway.

For Labor Day weekend, we went up to my parents' house in Maine, which is perched in a dense forest on a steep cliff overlooking a tidal river. It's an area that boaters and retirees love, but from my perspective, it's not ideal as a vacation house. I find it a little frustrating to drive all the way to the ocean and not go swimming. This part of the Maine coastline is frigid and rocky. Never in the twenty years my parents have owned this house have I seen anyone go swimming in this area.

We go up a couple of times a year just because it's an enjoyable getaway, and the kids still find novelty in going to sleep at night in a different house, one with a view of the water, of lobster boats sliding past, and of seals sunning on the rocks. Tim's birthday is in September, and rather than have a party in honor of turning nine, he asked if he could invite his best friend Austin up to Maine with us for Labor Day weekend.

Being there with our two kids plus Austin made me feel middle-aged, but not in a bad way: strangely, in a really *great* way. Rick and I had been coming up to the Maine house since we were just dating, often with friends and then with the kids when they were very small. Being there with our five-year-old and our eight-year-old who was celebrating turning nine by bringing a friend along made me feel like things were getting easier for us as parents, like the days of ceaseless baby- and toddler-tending were finally over. Maybe this was the halcyon phase of parenting, I thought more than once: tucked securely between baby-care and teenage woes.

On Saturday night, Rick produced a clambake of jaw-dropping proportions. The boys couldn't get enough of it: the saltiness, the seafood, the squirty mess, the buttery drips. Holly and I tired of the meal halfway through and went upstairs for her bath, but Rick, Tim and Austin sat at the table out on the porch for about two hours, prying meat out of the lobster tails and dipping clams into dishes of melted butter. I was impressed with the effort Rick put forth, and Tim was utterly delighted.

Tim's running log: Sun 9/2, 1 PM. Day 22. 1.2 miles. Fun and easy even though there are real steep hills here.

As we ran in Maine that weekend, Tim gave a lengthy disquisition on how that particular kind of terrain – packed dirt – was his favorite kind for running. It amused me that he already had a favorite kind of terrain after just three weeks as a runner, but it reminded me that kids tend to take themselves seriously; it's only later that we learn to doubt our abilities, to question our authenticity, to think the way I so often do: *You can't really be a runner just because you go running a lot. You aren't really a writer just because you publish articles. Having well-behaved children doesn't make you a great parent.*

Later that day, we boated into the village of Wiscasset, and Tim drove the boat nearly the whole way. He seemed so mature and capable, and it reminded me that many of his personality wrinkles will iron themselves out as he grows older because he simply likes being capable and in control. As a preschooler, he didn't enjoy playing with other kids until they started games with rules, like baseball; he didn't like kindergarten, but was happy in first grade because they started having desks and homework.

He's a kid who loves organized structure, which makes me think if I had suggested he go running with me once in a while, on a casual basis, it never would have happened. It was the rigidity of the streak that he found so attractive.

Tim's running log: Wed 9/5, 6:40 PM. Day 25. 1.3 miles. Up to soccer fields and back. Easy, nothing special to say about it.

On the first day of school, we always walk. I made plans to go into the office late so that I could do the ceremonial stroll with the kids. Holly was up an hour before dawn using the bathroom, and said to me as she headed back to bed, "The next time I wake up, it'll be my first day of kindergarten!"

I was so thankful that she was happy about it. I couldn't imagine how difficult and heartbreaking it would be to cope with a reticent child. When I dropped the kids off later that morning, there was the sound of screaming and crying from the school plaza, and at first I assumed it was a baby or much younger sibling who just didn't want to be dragged along for whatever reason, but then I became increasingly convinced that it was actually a kindergartener.

That was disturbing. If I were the parent, I'd be tempted to just turn around with the child and go home until his mind changed. I felt so fortunate that Holly and Tim were both, in their

24

own ways, enthusiastic about school. Holly said at the end of the day, "I can't *wait* to go back tomorrow!"

Tim's running log: Fri 9/7, 6:10 PM. Day 27. 1.2 miles. Warm. Breezy.

Tim often insisted that people in cars who passed us as we were out running stared at him. He claimed they were surprised to see someone so young out running. Though I didn't think it was all that remarkable a sight, it was fine with me if he derived motivation from the belief that other people were impressed by him.

I was guilty of that myself. I love to get credit from other people for running. Once when my friend Nicole and I went out for a run while Tim and her son had a baseball game, I said, "We can end the loop at the ball field," and she said "Oh no, then everyone will see us when we look gross!"

It amused me that she wanted to avoid being seen; by contrast, I love it when people say "Oh wow, did you just go running?" It definitely hearkens back to my having been such a bad athlete all my life. I find it remarkably gratifying whenever people are impressed by anything I can do in terms of physical exertion or coordination.

Tim's running log: Tues 9/11, 6:15 PM. Day 31. 1.2 miles. Cool and breezy, rain just ended. Big puddles. Very nice run, lots of talking. We've completed one month! We are going out for ice cream sundaes to celebrate.

September 11th. The date whose name sounds... sacrosanct. The date that has no name of its own, the way Christmas, Labor Day, Martin Luther King Day do, but will forever be called September 11th. Running as the sun covered the pastures with lemon-yellow light that morning, I was so aware of how similar the day just dawning was to the original September

25

11th, the one the date will forever connote. That too was a beautiful, bright, sunny, early autumn day.

I went running that day too, not first thing in the morning but after, midafternoon, at the point where I could no longer sit staring at the TV. I remember coming home after dropping Tim off at daycare that morning, going straight into the family room where Rick had the TV on, hoping to make sense of the bewildering news report I'd just heard on the car radio. I remember sinking down on a chair with my fall jacket still on and my car keys in hand, and realizing two hours later that I was still wearing my jacket and holding my car keys.

And then I remember finally dragging myself out of the chair later still, eating a sandwich for lunch, putting on my running clothes. I asked Rick if he thought it was offensive for me to go running, but I didn't listen to his answer. I knew it might be offensive to some people. To neighbors looking out of their windows, to cars passing by, maybe even to Rick himself.

"I just need to get out," I said. I just needed to run away from the news, from the TV, from the sound of sirens on TV. I was surprised later in the week when our minister, also a runner, said in a sermon that it took several days before she could bear to put on her running shoes; it felt too frivolous to her.

"Running was all I *could* do that afternoon," I confessed to her.

As the sixth anniversary drew near, Rick and Tim watched a news special about September 11th. On that date in 2001, Tim was just a few days shy of his third birthday, and I thought he'd remember forever the TV images of the planes flying into the tower, and the horrible unhappy days that followed. But he actually doesn't remember it at all. Six years later, walking into the playroom and seeing the image of a burning skyscraper on TV, I was momentarily stunned. "What happened?" I asked Rick, feeling frozen. "It's not current," he said, repeating it to try to disrupt my stupor. "It's footage from 2001. It's a documentary."

I thought it was too scary for Tim to watch, but Rick felt he was ready – ready to learn about this critical part of his own era, his own history.

"Just stop watching if you get too scared," I told Tim as the sound of ceaseless police sirens rose in the background from the TV. "Come find me and we'll do something else."

"I'm fine with it," Tim said resolutely.

And Rick was right; it is part of Tim's history, his era. He knows we're at war, and he knows or at least can recite my explanation of how there's no connection between the terrorist attacks and the war in Iraq but that President Bush wants people to think there is. He's not afraid of more terrorist attacks, probably because New York City is so remote to him.

September 11th of 2007, six years later, we headed out for a run at the crack of dawn, and oh what a beautiful morning to be out. The sky was just brightening, and after two days of rain, we could already see that it was going to be a clear, sunny day. Mostly, on that day, I wanted Tim to have that feeling of utter well-being that runners get on an absolutely perfect day. He knew it was a beautiful day, but of course he didn't feel the same sense of worship for it that I did, because he didn't realize how many not-beautiful days there would be, or even what it meant that we'd just reached another yearly September 11th.

INTERVIEW WITH
DAN SHAUGHNESSY
He's a streak runner – but not the registered kind
by Nancy Shohet West

Dan Shaughnessy is not interested in being listed by the United States Running Streak Association. He didn't even know it existed. And technically, they wouldn't be interested in him either, because he occasionally lets an hour of vigorous basketball or twenty minutes of lap swimming stand in for his daily run. Not permitted, according to USRSA guidelines.

Shaughnessy doesn't care. A sports columnist for the *Boston Globe* who has been named Massachusetts Sportswriter of the Year seven times and selected repeatedly as one of American's top-ten sports columnists by the Associated Press, he started his streak on the most popular day of the year for starting a streak: New Year's Day. New Year's Day of 1983, to be exact.

"It was your typical resolution," he says. "I was feeling fat and out of shape. My family tends to be overweight, and I had just turned 30, and I was starting to feel out of shape myself. So I put on my running shoes and ran a mile. Since that day in 1983, with exactly four exceptions, I've run a mile every single day, or very occasionally done the equivalent workout in basketball or swimming instead. I've done it with no interruptions since 1994."

Shaughnessy is no marathoner or distance runner. He's a miler, and a slow miler, at that. "People always ask me if I'm ever going to run farther. I'm not," he declares. "I know it takes me a little over ten minutes to run one mile, so I set my watch and that's it. Sometimes I have to use a treadmill instead of getting outside, and then I set the treadmill for one mile. I like to get it over with first thing in the morning. No breakfast, nothing, just up and go. If I don't do it then, it just bugs me, thinking about it."

First thing in the morning isn't always an option, though, especially for someone in his profession. Covering sports for a national newspaper, he travels regularly throughout the world, and the list of where he's covered his daily mile is a resume in itself. "The beaches on Santa Monica. Deeley Plaza in Dallas. New Orleans. The Bronx. Athens, Sydney, Barcelona, Paris, Rome. The Olympics, the World Series, the Superbowl. When I was traveling to Sydney for the 2000 Olympics, I wasn't quite sure what day it was after we crossed the International Date Line. I ran on a treadmill at a hotel in Seoul, but due to the 18-hour time difference, I kind of felt like I'd lost a day."

And when his young daughter was being treated for leukemia, he would wait each day until she fell asleep and then ran from the entrance to Children's Hospital half a mile down Brookline Avenue and back.

Like all streak runners, Shaughnessy has his share of crazy got-to-get-the-run-in stories.

"Once my wife and I overslept at a hotel in New York. When I woke up, I was due at Yankee Stadium to cover a game. I ended up going running through Manhattan that night at 1:30 a.m. for the day that had just ended, and then going five hours later for the day that was just beginning. Naturally, people asked me why I didn't just do two miles at once and cover both days."

Not only has he run throughout the world, but if he adds up 25 years of daily miles, Shaughnessy points out that from a distance perspective, he's gone across the country and back. "Like Forrest Gump," he says.

You can't work up a lot of Zen mindset on a ten-minute mile; nor is that Shaughnessy's intent. "Overweight runs in my family, but my weight has stayed at just under 200 for all these years," he says. My cardiovascular health, my blood pressure and cholesterol levels, they're all great.

"I've run with broken bones in my foot and torn hamstrings," Shaughnessy says. "Even at my best, I'm a weak, slow runner. It's a joke in my family what a bad runner I am. But I get out there for my daily mile. Honor the streak. It's all about honoring the streak."

CHAPTER 2

September 12 – October 11, 2007

Tim's running log: Wed 9/12, 6:05 AM. Day 32. 1.8 miles. We watched the sunlight spread over the road. Nice mild air.

Tim and Holly attend the same K-8 school I attended at their age. Sometimes when I'm on campus to pick them up, I make an excuse to go into the buildings, just to inhale the familiar smells and see what unexpected memories come back. There's a certain aroma of furnace and cleaning solution and turkey sandwiches from hundreds of lunchboxes that greets me every time I walk into the first-grade hallway, and I'm six years old again, safe and happy, at school for the day.

It's at moments like this that I can't quite grasp the impossibility of time travel. It seems that I'm so close from a sensory standpoint to myself as a six-year-old that surely I could walk out the door and climb onto a bus and ride it two miles to my old neighborhood and go into the house we lived in before my parents moved to the farm and find my mother heating soup for lunch.

Both kids were happy at school that fall, which is one of the greatest blessings I could hope for. They liked their teachers and had plenty of friends: Tim's were mostly kids he had known for two or three years now, Holly's were mostly new to her since the start of the year. I can get unhappy about things at work or our financial picture or even various permutations of family dynamics,

31

but the fact that my children love to go to school every day means the world to me.

Tim's running log: Thurs 9/13, 6:15 PM. Day 33. 1 mile. Nice running through the cemetery. Very short run.

One morning we ran along the gravel path that runs through the old cemetery near the Town Center. Tim commented, "It's sort of neat to see all the names." Then he asked, "When I die, can I be buried with Ba and Vicon?"

Those are his two beloved stuffed animals. Ba is a ragged pale green frog Tim has had since he was a year old, and Vicon is a gray elephant wearing a mortarboard that he received as a present when he graduated from preschool. He sleeps with both animals clutched to his chest.

I answered that as far as I was concerned, he could, but quite likely I wouldn't be the one in charge of the event. Then he asked why a particular gravesite had freshly dug earth and floral arrangements but no gravestone. I explained that it can take a while for a gravestone to be carved, and often it doesn't arrive until some time has passed since the burial. He asked if I thought my paternal grandmother had her gravestone yet. I said yes, considering she died four years ago. He asked if I thought my other grandmother, who died a year later, had one yet. I said no because she was cremated. He asked what that meant, and I explained about ashes, and he asked how they make the ashes, so I explained that as well. Then, naturally, he wanted to know whether first they make sure you're dead, and if so, how. He didn't sound frightened, just genuinely curious. What a strange conversation, and yet what a perfect conversation starter: going running in a cemetery.

Tim turned nine years old on September 15. I always have mixed feelings about the month of his birthday. It so poignantly brings back the days around his birth, which was such a complicated and ambivalent time for me. I was thrilled to be having my first child, and the birth itself wasn't difficult. But for weeks afterwards, I suffered from postpartum depression that I was too embarrassed to tell anyone about, or to ask for help, even though it was obvious to me that something was wrong.

He was very much planned and very much wanted. We'd been married for six years and I was almost thirty-two years old. My job as a copywriter for a travel company had given both Rick and me four years' worth of exotic travel opportunities throughout Europe and even to Kenya, but we were ready to give that up and it just seemed like the time had come.

So Tim arrived, healthy and perfect. And I remember that even as the nurse was giving us our discharge instructions forty-six hours after we checked into the hospital, I had tears streaming down my cheeks, not because I actually felt depressed yet but because I knew it was coming, just waiting for me as soon as I left the comfortable care of the maternity ward.

Still, I couldn't make myself say the words: Something's wrong, I need help, I can't cope. I told the nurse I was having post-delivery cramping, and she gave me a strong dose of ibuprofen. I held my baby and let the panic wash over me in waves.

At home, I cried my way through the first two weeks. The first evening, when Tim was three days old, my parents brought dinner over. I sat at the table, staring at Mom and Dad and Rick through what felt like a leaden veil. It was just the same way I felt those first few evenings at college when my hallmates and I would go to the cafeteria together. Sitting there, frozen on the outside, sick on the inside, thinking "I can't do this. I just can't."

It went on like that for days. We lived in another town at the time, but my parents lived close by enough that they dropped by often. One afternoon my mother and I were sitting on the patio on a warm fall day, Tim in his carrier dozing, and my mother said, "I think you should talk to your doctor. I think you seem depressed."

It was the first time anyone had noticed, but I fought it. "Mom, I'm fine," I said with my throat squeezed up with tears.

"Everyone feels this way sometimes." That was what all my baby-care books said: everyone feels this way sometimes.

But I felt that way *all* the time. One evening I finally said to Rick, "I feel like something is wrong with me."

"Physically or mentally?" he asked.

The idea of something being wrong physically seemed so tantalizing. If only. If only I could say "I'm bleeding profusely and need emergency care." If only I could check back into the hospital and be taken care of again. But that wasn't the case. I was healthy and so was my perfect little son, whom I adored through my leaden unhappiness.

What saved me was a group for new mothers based at the hospital where I delivered. I attended it for the first time when Tim was three weeks old. It was a drop-in group with no specific starting or ending date, so it was open to mothers at a variety of stages. Tim was the youngest baby there that day; the oldest was nearly six months. Some of the mothers had been attending for months and knew each other well; they sat on the floor, spreading blankets in front of them and letting their babies roll around, giving them rattles or teething rings to reach for. I gazed at those mothers, unable to imagine feeling that cheerful and playful.

When it was my turn to introduce, I said "I'm Nancy...this is Tim...he's three weeks old...and I feel completely at sea. He's healthy and perfect and I have no idea how to cope."

"Hmmm...." the facilitator, a social worker named Robin, said. "Anyone here able to relate to that?"

And then what seemed like a miraculous thing happened: all these other women, these nicely dressed and well groomed, smiling, laughing, baby-cuddling women, exclaimed that they had felt *exactly* the same way at three weeks. One woman admitted crying over a comment her father-in-law made about nursing; another told of wanting to kill her husband in cold blood because he asked her if she was planning to make dinner. It turned out they all had felt that way, and they had all gotten through it.

"Nancy, if you need help, I promise you we can find help," Robin said at last. "But I don't think you will. I think you're going to be okay."

And I was. But it took a little while longer. Afterwards, I felt apologetic toward Tim; I felt like I'd missed out on his first few weeks of life. And September still brings me back there. I'm so thankful every year on his birthday that I have him, and that he's so healthy and happy and well off in countless ways. But I also remember how I felt that September when he was new.

Tim's running log: Sun 9/16, 11 AM. Day 36. 1.6 miles. With Nicole and Austin. Very fun.

Tim still wanted more names to add to our guest list, so he was delighted when my friend Nicole, who is Tim's best friend Austin's mother, said she would run with us one morning. Then Austin decided he would give it a try as well.

Tim's friends tend to be strong athletes. At their age, boys who like sports tend to band together; even without any training, a run of a mile or so isn't much of a strain for any of them. The two boys loped side by side in front and the two of us moms jogged behind. Nicole and I talked about helicopter parents and soccer teams and our workplaces. I would have loved to know what Tim and Austin were discussing – they ran steadily and conversed the whole time – but I couldn't hear them, and when I asked Tim afterwards, he just shrugged.

Nicole and I had known each other for only four years, but we had done a lot of things together with our boys in that time. We'd taken them to the zoo and the beach together; coordinated sleepovers for the kids at each other's houses; stayed at each other's vacation homes; gone to birthday parties and baseball games and class plays.

Ever since Tim and Austin first became preschool buddies, I'd enjoyed trying to picture how they'll grow together through the years. I could imagine them egging each other on with junior high pranks, playing sports together in high school, finding their way to each other's houses within hours after getting home during college vacations. Their differences were so obvious – Austin a tall, wide-shouldered, all-American blond type, Tim wiry and dark-haired; Austin calm, cheerful and easygoing, Tim intense and serious – they were like typecasted buddies in a movie or sitcom. I pictured them far into the future confiding in each other in the not-very-verbal way that boys do about girlfriends (or boyfriends) and college classes and job searches and promotions. Maybe they'd keep running together too.

Three days after his birthday, Tim had his yearly checkup with the nurse practitioner who has always been the primary medical caretaker for both kids. She opined that it was a fine idea for him to go running every day. After all the online controversy, it was a relief to hear a medical professional affirm my belief that a boy who runs under two miles a day is not ruining his bones and muscles. As I kept saying, under two miles is equivalent to a vigorous soccer or basketball game. But it was good to feel for once that maybe I wasn't doing the Irresponsible Parent thing.

During the appointment, the nurse practitioner told us that she was pregnant with her fourth child. Her youngest was Holly's age. So: a new baby when the youngest had just started kindergarten. I could not imagine wanting that, but it impressed me that she did. I feel like such a curmudgeon around people like her, because I am so grateful to be beyond that baby-tending point. I find life with the kids so much more fun the way they are now.

As Tim and I racked up the days of our streak and Holly vacillated between finding her groove in kindergarten and reverting to baby talk at home, the world went on around us as well. The war in Iraq dragged on, one casualty after another: not just deaths but injuries and heartbreak of all kinds. I listened to a woman on NPR talking about how hard the war was on families.

36

"Children are being raised without their mothers or fathers," she said. "Men come home to insufficient resources for their battle wounds and their post-traumatic stress alike."

Mostly, she just emphasized what a strain deployment puts on families, and it reminded me yet again of how cushy life is here for us. There are mothers – and fathers too – raising a child while the other parent is away long-term in combat. The parent at home has to worry about making ends meet and taking care of the children and staying employed and also the soldier's safety and well-being. It must be unbelievably stressful. It made me want to scream when Rick would complain about something like a broken computer monitor.

But it was good to be reminded. We had enough trouble juggling if one of us went away for a night or two, and that was just a matter of managing the practical details; it didn't even take into account the emotional burden these families are under. I thought of all the wives whose husbands were gone for months on end, or the reverse, children whose mothers had to leave. Children for whom both parents had to leave and they stayed with relatives. It was so disturbing to me, and yet it was so important to think about.

Tim's running log: Thurs 9/20, 7 PM. Day 40. 1.1 miles. Good run, had fun.

Running past a dead squirrel in the road one evening, Tim went on a tirade of sorts about how much roadkill there is in Carlisle. I explained that this is just a town with a lot of trees, a lot of wildlife, and also a lot of traffic.

He became maudlin, the way kids his age are wont to do over dead wildlife. "But it's just so sad!" he intoned.

"Tim, there are a lot of animals around here and a lot of cars! It just happens sometimes!" I said. "No one likes it, but – "

"Can't people be more careful?" he demanded.

"Well, when you're driving, you *are* careful, but sometimes you just can't help it!"

"It's not fair," he announced again. "Just tell me one thing: Have you ever seen a *squirrel* run over a *person*?"

He lives on a farm; it's not like he wasn't familiar with the life-and-death cycle of animals.

Carlisle Mosquito – September 28, 2007
The tribe has voted — and they all disagree with
me about snack-free soccer
by Nancy Shohet West

"You're going straight to that special circle of Hades reserved for bad soccer moms," I muttered to myself as I clicked on "Send." "See that long branch? That's a limb. Hear that buzzing sound? That's a chainsaw, cutting it off behind you."

I was feeling reckless on that late evening last week, as I sat at my computer. I had just sent off an e-mail to all the parents whose kids are on my son's fall soccer team, suggesting that maybe we could skip the seasonal ritual of making up a schedule to provide group snacks for each game.

By the next morning, I was almost hyperventilating as I turned on my computer. Had I been voted off the island? Drummed out of the PTA? Would I find "BAD MOM" written on my car in shaving cream when I went outside?

No. None of those. Perhaps I was the only parent on the team — maybe even in the league — who did not feel that a snack schedule was necessary, but I was being treated kindly. There were no repercussions, other than my own lingering questions about why I'm the only one who feels this way.

Actually, I'm not quite the *only* one. My friend Terry sent me an essay from the *New York Times* several months ago about this very thing. So there's one parent in New York with the same sentiments. But New York feels very far away right now, if it's just the two of us.

Ever since my son started playing soccer at the age of four, the season has always begun with a parent circulating a snack sign-up list. It seems to be a given that kids need their halftime snacks. And although I'm not advocating for undernourishing our children, I just want to make a case for the fact that the average soccer game for this age group is about 75 minutes long. As long as the kids bring their water bottles and stay hydrated, do we really have to assume that they cannot go 75 minutes without graham crackers and apple slices?

Or might it in fact be the case that learning to go an hour and a quarter without eating is yet another step in acquiring the self-discipline required for sports?

By contrast, we just finished two consecutive seasons of snack-free baseball — spring and summer. The subject simply never came up. Occasionally, kids would arrive at a game straight from another activity, hungry, and would pull out their own snack to eat before play began. I never heard any other kid express jealousy or demand to know where his portion of the snack was. The kids understood.

Of course, I respect the fact that there are some children who really should have snacks in the midst of a game, either for reasons of metabolism, blood-sugar imbalances or personal preference. But if that's the case, then having parents take turns providing for the team deprives us all of a teaching opportunity. It seems to me that the process of choosing a sensible snack, finding the right way to package it and remembering to bring it along is a fine skill to include among the benefits of organized sports. It's yet another way of learning responsibility. Kids who forget a snack once and regret it are likely to remember the next time.

My daughter's kindergarten teacher sent home a summary last week describing what had happened in the first ten days of school. She had surveyed the kids about what they liked best so far – and what they liked least. Somewhat to my surprise, the single entry that came up most in the "like least" category was, in the kindergartners' words, "trying to remember everything we need to bring to school every day!" Backpacks, bus tags, lunch money for long days, snacks for short days, library books, sneakers for gym.

The kindergarteners are right – it *is* difficult to remember all of life's details. I still forget things I need for work when I leave in the morning. And yet I believe that these simple organizational processes are among the most important skills that children learn in grade school. Kids who have to remember a snack for soccer are having yet another chance each week to make sure they are well prepared for the event at hand.

As for the response to my suggestion, a couple of parents eventually wrote back to say "I think snacks are important"; others simply signed up to bring snacks, without comment. And I should mention that in my initial e-mail, I also signed up to provide snacks on the first available game day myself, not wanting anyone to misconstrue my point and respond along the lines of "Well then, *you* don't have to do it!"

But it turned out there was a different moral to the story of the snack e-mail. No one has banished me from the soccer field or crossed me off the PTA membership list. My parenting peers are more patient, more understanding and more flexible than I had given them credit for. The lesson to me, ultimately, is a reminder that intelligent minds can disagree but friendships need not be lost over it. That's a good lesson, at my age.

Meanwhile, I guess the kids get a few more years before they'll be required to meet their own midgame nutritional needs.

Tim's running log: Sat 9/29, 8:30 AM. Day 49. 2.2 miles. Sunny and cool. Our first run over 2 miles! Eric M. did the last ½ mile with us.

After seven weeks, I convinced Tim to try adding a little distance. On a hot Saturday morning, we did a 2.2-mile run, and Tim was exuberant when it was over.

When we reached our door, I said "You did it, Tim! Two-point-two miles!" and I thought his face would split in half with glee. I was so happy to see *him* so happy, and with such a sense of accomplishment. All day, I could just tell there was a little flame of pride burning within him, knowing that he had met a new physical challenge.

I've had that feeling so many times myself. I've never played baseball or soccer the way he does, so this was in a way the first time I could really relate to the sense of excitement he was experiencing over an athletic accomplishment. It was a nice thing to be able to share.

Being in Tim's classroom on Parents' Night, I was so conscious of the fact that I just want this phase of my life to go on for a very long time. With Tim in third grade and Holly in kindergarten, both kids were at wonderful stages. And it wasn't just the kids themselves; it was the whole milieu that surrounded them.

I just love the feel of a second- or third-grade classroom, the way everything is so focused on learning and creativity. There's something still so *pure* about everything concerning grade school. Though you always have to worry about your kids' behavior and whether they are fitting in effectively and happily, in grade school the circumstances just seem so ideal.

By middle school there's so much to worry about as far as their behavior and comportment, and then from there it's on to worrying about their future, whether they'll get in to college, whether in our case we'll even know how and where to apply to college, whether we'll be able to pay for it, and so on. But grade school...grade school feels perfect.

Tim's running log: Sun 9/30, 5:30 PM. Day 50. 2.1 miles. We went to the Cranberry Bog and saw a lot of people out walking. It was a pretty run.

Tim's running log: Tues 10/2, 6 AM. Day 52. 1.2 miles. Cool, dark, early morning. Fresh air, comfortable pace.

I was really pleased with how easily Tim had taken to running. He seemed to love it almost as much as I did, and he was starting to take pride in trying increasing distances, which was nice for me. My favorite runs in the past had always been in the three- to five-mile range, and although I was having fun seeing Tim develop as a runner, I couldn't help hoping he'd reach my level as far as distances eventually. Running for less than twenty minutes hardly seems worth changing clothes for.

Although becoming a regular runner had improved his attitude toward running, it hadn't had the widespread changes elsewhere in his life that I had hoped to see. He still watched too much TV and spent too much time playing video games.

And he could still be so *lazy*, in my estimation. Although he had proved himself able to run more than two miles at a stretch and refused to miss a day of running, he still wouldn't tie his own running shoes. When it was time to head out for a run, he would ask me to find him a pair of socks and then sit on the bench in the mudroom until I tied his shoes for him. The kid who could probably run more than three miles by that time – which I suspected was something no other third grader at his school currently did – wouldn't *tie his own shoes*.

Tim's running log: Sat, 10/ 6, 5 PM. Day 56. 3 miles. Lots of people were out walking and some were speaking French. My mom said they were Canadian tourists.

43

Finally, we did our first three-mile run, driving to Concord and parking at the Old North Bridge, a historical landmark known for its Revolutionary War ties. Tim was not accustomed to running on a flat paved roadway, and he was elated by how easy it was. I was elated that we were out on the road for thirty-seven minutes. As I said to Tim afterwards, for the first time, we were doing a run I might actually choose to do by myself.

And that seemed so significant to me, because for so long, one of my goals in parenting had been to raise my children up to my level. When they were babies and toddlers, I felt like I was paying my dues with playing on the floor and going to Music Together and watching clowns perform at birthday parties and clapping for the kids when they peed in the potty. I spent so many years tailoring my preferences to their abilities. And always it was with the dream that someday *they'd* be able to do what *I* wanted to do, rather than always vice versa.

But gradually, Tim and Holly were starting to do things that felt like they were on *my* level: eating foods I would choose, reading books I liked, going for bike rides, and at last, going running. And by doing his first run of over thirty minutes, Tim did a run I would actually choose to do even if I were by myself. Which was huge, as far as I was concerned.

Tim's running log: Sun, 10/ 7. Day 57, 1 PM. 1.4 miles. The leaves are starting to change colors.

In a town about fifteen miles from us, a six-year-old girl collapsed and died during Saturday morning soccer practice. Six-year-olds at soccer: what could be more everyday than that? And now a family had lost its little girl, and a community was coping with everyone's shock and grief, and dozens of young kids and parents who witnessed the whole thing were probably experiencing all kinds of acute stress symptoms.

I could so easily imagine the same thing happening in Carlisle – because it so easily *could* happen – and I kept thinking about how everyone would be grieving and miserable all season, maybe all year. I kept thinking of how if that happened to one of Holly's friends, I would dwell constantly on the family, wondering how they could bear the pain.

Of course, it could happen to one of my kids too, but I found it actually so much harder to think of it happening to someone else. At least if it happened to you, you wouldn't have to think of anyone else. You could immerse yourself in the grief and not *wonder* how they could possibly cope.

When I was in college, there was a twelve-year-old boy from Carlisle who went into cardiac arrest at the end of his driveway after a run. I worried about that happening to Tim, knowing that I would have to deal not only with the grief but also the guilt and the blame if he died as a result of running. It was almost a reason not to run with him, and yet we were enjoying our running together so very much.

Tim's running log: Wed, Oct 10, 6:15 PM. Day 60. 2.1 miles. We are about to reach two months!!

CHAPTER 3

October 12 – November 12, 2007

October was gorgeous that year, as it almost always is in New England, with every day like a scene from a calendar, trees flaming yellow and red against Wedgewood blue skies. On a quintessential autumn day, a Saturday of bright sunshine and crisp air, with kids playing soccer and cyclists gliding through a veil of cascading leaves, a neighbor of ours, Kate, dropped by to tell me she had been diagnosed with inoperable breast cancer.

Inoperable *breast* cancer? was, bizarrely, my first, though mercifully silent, reaction. I thought breast cancer was always operable these days. Lots of people recover from breast cancer. Especially women my age. Women in their forties. Women raising young children. Women like Kate.

Kate and her family lived on a horse farm down the road from us. They had moved there the previous autumn, and we didn't see a lot of them, but we had come to really enjoy their company in the short time we'd been neighbors. Kate and her daughters liked to ride their horses through the woods to our house, and sometimes they dismounted and stayed for a visit. In just eleven months, their presence had become a regular part of our lives.

And now: inoperable cancer. In the mother of two grade school aged children. The news made it hard for me to breathe. And I could only imagine how it had been for Kate, and for her husband, finding out about it a couple of weeks earlier.

"I still feel absolutely fine. They'll treat it with drugs," she said quite calmly. "It's like a cat and mouse game: the doctor says they just keep chasing it with different drugs. They can't get rid of the cancer, but they can just keep trying whatever might work to keep it from growing."

Always, the question: *What do you say? How do you respond?* "You know we want to do anything we can to help," I said. "You know that you must never hesitate to tell us what we can do for you."

Kate was so poised, so collected. I was the one who wanted to scream with the awfulness of it. "I figure it just means I now know what I'll probably die of," she remarked. "Anyway, I wanted you to know."

If we hadn't met them, I thought to myself when Kate left, *this would still be happening but we wouldn't know about it. It would be someone else's awful story, one we hadn't heard.*

The old tree-in-the-forest problem: How do we go on living our lives, knowing that awful things happen to good people all the time, whether we know about it or not?

Tim's running log: Fri 10/12, 6 AM. Day 62. 2 miles. Colder in the morning this week.

I reminded myself often that the goals of the streak were 1) To get Tim to spend less time playing video games; 2) To get Tim to have a less grumpy disposition; 3) To introduce Tim to the bliss of being a runner, which is indescribable and impossible to replicate through any other means. In general, when I stopped to evaluate, it seemed that after two months I'd failed miserably in #1 and couldn't say I'd seen a great deal of progress in #2, but #3 had so far been a success. My parents told me that from their perspective, Tim talked about running all the time. It's not that he had low self-esteem before – and he was already a good athlete – but now he was more engaged than ever in something productive, quantitative, ambitious. And it was good to see what that did for him.

As the Red Sox raced onward toward another World Series win – their second this century, having gone 86 years without a championship prior to 2004 – the *Boston Globe* assigned me a story on a lab in the engineering department at the University of Massachusetts in Lowell where Major League baseballs undergo quality control testing.

The assignment caused us to have our closest call yet to missing out on our run. On a Saturday in mid-October, with the Red Sox pitted against the Cleveland Indians in the playoff games, Tim and I planned to do a midafternoon run and then head to Rick's parents' house in Lakeville, which is an hour south of Carlisle, for their anniversary celebration.

As we were on our way out the door, I noticed that there was a message on my cell phone: an editor whose name I didn't recognize wanted me to call the weekend desk immediately.

I did, and he said that the article was scheduled to run the next day but needed another crucial element: a quote from someone associated with Major League Baseball.

Beat reporters work under that kind of pressure all the time – with a half-hour to go before deadline, having to track down a head of state or some other major figure for a quote – but the kinds of stories I normally write don't work like that at all. I'm strictly a features, human-interest writer. I write stories about the most everyday people doing things just unusual enough to make them interesting. I wrote about a group for mothers whose children had severe food allergies. I wrote about six suburban middle-aged dads who perform at parties as a garage band. I wrote about the fact that in Carlisle's incoming kindergarten class of seventy kids, there were six sets of twins and one set of triplets. I write fun, interesting, easy stories whose subjects are local, everyday people who are easy to track down and happy to talk to me.

But now I had ninety minutes to reach the commissioner of baseball on a Saturday afternoon.

"I'm not that kind of reporter!" I wanted to protest to the city editor. Which would be a little bit like saying "I'm not the kind of actor who tries out for lead roles!": remarkably self-defeating. So I scrambled, calling Fenway Park's press office and reaching someone who gave me the number of the MLB press office who gave me the cell phone number of the chief MLB spokesman, who was in Denver at the Rockies playoffs game.

By the time I had my quote – which was something benign like "The University of Massachusetts provides a great service to Major League baseball by quality-testing all of the baseballs we use" – not only had Tim and I missed our run but we were already an hour late to Rick's parents' house. So we packed up our running clothes and left, figuring we could run once we got there.

But that turned out not to be practical. It was seven o'clock and the other guests, including Rick's grandparents, who were both in their eighties, had been waiting for us since six. We couldn't just breeze in, greet them all, and then go out for a run while they grew ever hungrier. So we ate, and Tim and I did a mile-long loop after dinner.

In the end, I felt a little like I lived through a stress dream. The kind of dream where a major city editor calls and says he needs an MLB quote within the next hour, and you think "How the *hell* am I gonna do that?" I came through, and I knew I should have been proud, but instead I just felt kind of professionally traumatized.

Fall is my favorite time of year. I love autumn weather and the brisk, back-to-school energy that comes with it. But some years there are challenging school transition issues to cope with, and it turned out this was one of them. Ever since birth, Holly has

50

been a happy, cheerful little person, agreeable and compliant. But perhaps it was the anxieties associated with starting kindergarten, or perhaps my concerns about her being the youngest and smallest in the class were proving to be well-founded. By mid-fall, she seemed to be ending every single day with a tantrum, crying and whining when it was time to brush her teeth and put on pajamas.

Exasperated, I resolved one evening after yet another tantrum to try something different. Rather than taking a tough line and insisting that she do what I asked, I simply left her bedroom light on, closed her door and walked away. After about ten minutes of silence, Holly opened her door and silently came to me for a hug. I realized that left on her own, she had worked it out inside her head and everything was fine then. For once, my impulses seemed to work. For once I had a decent strategy: walk away and it will pass. And it did.

Tim's running log: Sun 10/14, 11 AM. Day 64. 3.4 miles. We did a longer run and it was no problem for me. Me and my mom were talking about school stuff.

While we were out on a run, Tim said he wanted to tell me about a rumor he'd heard at school.

"You tell me, and I'll tell you whether I think it's true or not," I said, symbolically if not literally holding my breath.

The so-called rumor turned out to be more of a ghost story. Because the pipes in the boys' room at school squeak, the boys were circulating a tale that a child had gotten stuck in the cabinetry and starved to death and was haunting the restroom.

I was all but certain it had generated organically and has nothing to do with the fact that nine months ago, in a suburban high school less than ten miles from us, a freshman was fatally stabbed by a mentally ill classmate in the boys' restroom, but Tim's story reminded me of that awful event. I spent the rest of the run thinking about how fragile and potentially frightening their childhoods are, and how glad I am that they are still spreading

51

ghost stories rather than fearing actual violence when they go off to school each day.

I was also glad Tim chose to tell me the so-called rumor. If we continued running together as he grew, was he likely to confide in me more? Would the solitude of being out on a run together, and the companionship, and the sheer sense of well-being that endorphins create, give us better mother-son communication than we would otherwise have? It did seem quite feasible at that moment.

Tim's journal
Oct. 16, 2007

Me and my mom are running every day! We run from 1 to as many miles as we want. When we started running I could only run a quarter of it now I can easily do the entire run. It all got started about two year ago, my mom wrote an article about a man who was just about to reach 30 years strait of running every day! About two months ago (when we started) my mom said...want to try to go running every day as long as we can? I said yes, and that's how it all began. My favorite time to go running is on the weekend because we try to increase our mileage! So far we're at 66 days and still going.

In May of 2006, having been away from full-time work since Holly's birth four years earlier, I was hired for the position of employee communications specialist at a biosciences company. My first year there was a really satisfying time. Worrying that I was unemployable after four years as a stay-at-home mom, I was relieved to get the job, and my manager seemed to value my skills. Writing for the company's internal website and newsletter didn't require too much creativity but posed an interesting challenge to my editorial abilities.

Many writers take day jobs in corporate communications or copywriting and continue with more creative pursuits in their off-hours. Since the kinds of stories I was writing for the *Globe* and other publications didn't usually require me to be on the spot at any particular time, the way news reporters have to be, I figured I could continue writing nights and weekends and find creative fulfillment that way even as my day job required me to write about scientific concepts like genome sequencing, chemical studies and advances in various kinds of environmental testing.

And in fact, it turned out to be a good balance. The dryness of the material I wrote about during the day fueled my creativity outside of work; I wrote more essays and feature stories during my first year of full-time work than I had for the four years I was home with the kids.

But after a year, my enthusiasm for the job had cooled. I worked closely with only one person, and that was Joan, my manager. When she first hired me, she had commented on how much we had in common. She was nearly twenty years older than me, but at my age she too had been an essayist and an aspiring journalist.

I think she believed I'd develop a passion for corporate writing the same way she had, but to me it remained a day job while the writing I was doing outside of work held far more interest. And I think Joan resented that, not because she thought it was disloyal to the company but because it highlighted the passion for writing that she herself had essentially sold out to the corporate world. She had once dreamed of doing the kind of writing I was doing; instead, she became a corporate communications executive, and I think my accomplishments, half-baked as they often seemed to me, still underscored for her the path not taken.

One day shortly after I started working for her, she gazed out the window and said, "You know what I sometimes think would be the greatest job in the world? Writing stories for the *Globe's* travel section!"

"I actually have a story coming out in the *Globe*'s travel section this Sunday," I said without thinking about it. That probably wasn't the most tactful response, in retrospect, but to me it would later serve as an accurate representation of our conflict. I didn't care enough about the biosciences; and my lack of interest, even though I was competent at the job, reminded her of the time when it wasn't her highest aspiration either.

Tim's running log: Sat 10/20, 3:30 PM. Day 70. 4 miles. We went to the Minuteman Bikeway to see if we could do four miles. We did it!

Pushing ourselves to build mileage, Tim and I ran four miles on the Minuteman Bikeway, a beautiful paved-over railroad route in an adjoining town. Unlike where we live, it's straight, flat and paved, so we tend to feel like we're sailing when we run there; plus we're surrounded by other runners, walkers, and in-line skaters, which makes it festive.

I was amazed at Tim's ability to run four miles completely unfazed. Like me, once he gets into the rhythm of it, he can go on forever. Well, mentally I still felt like that. Physically, it didn't always seem to be the case anymore. Because that was another reality that running with Tim was forcing me to face: while he was heading into his prime as a young athlete, I was past forty and starting to decline.

In my mind, I felt just like the runner I'd been at eighteen, but there was no question my body was changing. I ran slower, felt creakier, and had a much harder time maintaining my weight than I ever had before. A lot of my friends said the latter happened to them right around forty also.

But four miles on the Minuteman Bikeway was no trouble for either of us. Nonetheless, Tim brought his two favorite stuffed animals in the car for the drive to the trail and held them until it was time to get out.

I teased him about it, asking if when he runs the Boston Marathon someday, does he want Ba the Frog and Vicon the

Elephant at the starting line when he leaves, or waiting for him at the finish?

There were days when I felt like I had so much trouble connecting with Tim. We had a plan to have a portrait photographer do a photo shoot of Tim and Holly along with their cousins, so that we could give the portrait to Rick's parents for Christmas. As we planned it, I realized it was really important to me that Rick come to the sitting, for no other reason than that I was certain Tim would dig in his heels about something like "I won't smile" or "I won't sit next to Holly" and ruin everything, and I'd be powerless to fix it. I'm so terrible at managing his intransigence.

Rick is much better at dealing with the kids than I am. He's so rational and objective; he never lets the need to please them get in the way of a good decision. As a result, things don't get crazy when he's in charge. Only when I am, because I can't be as resolute or as rational as he can.

Tim's running log: Sun 10/21, 11 AM. Day 71. 2.2 miles. Tons of hills. We ran with Austin and Nicole but Austin didn't do the whole thing.

We ran again with Austin and Nicole, this time in their hilly neighborhood. Austin dropped out after a little over a mile, but Tim continued to lead the way while Nicole and I gabbed together behind him. I could so clearly imagine Tim and Austin in high school or even college, still running buddies. And yet when they're in high school or college I'll be remembering them as third graders, little boys with wiry legs, gabbing about Harry Potter and Red Sox players. Parenthood is funny that way. When they're little you look ahead; when they're older you look back.

When our local newspaper had a headline about taxes going up, I knew Rick was going to hit the roof. I thought seriously about hiding the paper from him that week – but then I told myself I'd rather he find out about it now than when the tax bill arrives.

As predicted, he did hit the roof; his exact words were "We just can't afford to live in this HOUSE." Those are the words that break my heart.

And yet knowing about Kate's diagnosis gave me such a different perspective. I'd long been in the habit of going outside just before bed every night to gaze at the sky and thank the universe for a safe, healthy, happy day. Inevitably, I'd then look out over the fields and forests that surrounded me and think to myself, *I just really don't want to have to leave here.* But with Kate's news, I kept answering myself, "Kate doesn't want to have to leave her farm either. But it might not be up to her. And it might not be up to you."

There are all sorts of ways we lose what we want. Foreclosure can force you out of your home; terminal illness can force you out of your entire life. None of us wants to leave here – whether it's the farm or the actual state of existence itself. But it's not always up to us, is it?

As darkness began to fall earlier, we ran often after dusk. One evening as a full moon rose, we ran up to the soccer fields; Tim marveled at the brightness of the moonlight shining on the soccer field. We could actually see our moon-shadows. It reminded me that among other things Tim is learning through this running-streak endeavor is a lot more about the natural world: how you can always orient yourself to the compass points if you can see the sun, for example; how long each phase of the moon appears to last; which stars and planets emerge visibly at what time.

He's so much more cognizant of the natural world than I was at his age. Or at almost any age, for that matter. I was so insecure as a kid. Would becoming a runner at the onset of adolescence have offset that? Surely it would. The kick of endorphins on a daily basis would have made a huge difference. I only hoped it might for Tim.

Tim's running log: Sat 10/ 27, 2 PM. Day 77. 4 miles. It's nice to run in the afternoon on weekends because afterwards we can rest.

Tim came up with a name for our running club. As we were heading home at the end of an after-dinner run one evening, he said, "Mom, the only thing that could break our streak now would be something like an earthquake."

"No, Tim," I replied, maternal pride battling good sense, "a fever like the one you had last spring when you had strep, or a stomach virus, could also end our streak."

"No, that would *not* end our streak," he retorted, indignant. "Ending our streak because of a fever or something like that would be if we were *babies*. And *we ain't no babies*."

The way he said it just cracked me up – like a lot of suburban boys his age, he could bring on the hip-hop posturing and urban street talk at will – but I'd never heard him say anything exactly like this before. So I said that should be our name: the "We Ain't No Babies Running Streak Club."

He commented it would be a better name for a rock band, but I pointed out that we don't have a rock band and we do have a running streak, so that would have to do for now.

Tim's running log: Wed 10/31, 6 AM. Day 81. 1.4 miles. My mom woke me up SO EARLY and I was SO TIRED. It's Halloween.

On Halloween day, I knew our only chance to run would be first thing in the morning since Tim was invited to go trick-or-treating with Austin and would be leaving before I got home from work. But it made for a moment I could hardly take pride in. Tim was so tired when I woke him up that morning. He never actually said "No, I don't want to get up!", but I still felt what I did bordered on cruelty; he was miserably sleepy and desperate to get back to bed but I coaxed him up anyway.

There just weren't any other options, and I knew he'd be disappointed if I'd let him sleep and then later he found out we wouldn't be able to go running that day. He all but sleepwalked his way downstairs and out the door, and whimpered throughout the whole run. I kept trying to engage him in conversation, but all he did was whimper in response.

When we were done, he took a bath, and was feeling better by breakfast time. The voices of my many online detractors were definitely chiming in my head with heavy sarcasm, though: "Way to go, obsessive-compulsive mom!"

GUEST RUNNERS AND THEIR HOMETOWNS 10/31/07
Eric M. - Carlisle, MA
Nicole P. - Carlisle, MA
Austin P. - Carlisle, MA
Sophie R. - Swarthmore, PA
Alyssa A. - Sandwich, MA

DOGS
Angus P. - Carlisle, MA

Tim's running log: Sat 11/3, 2:30 PM. Day 84. 4.2 miles. WE GOT SOAKED!! But it was funny and not that bad. My mom complained more than me.

As the first weekend of November began, the weather forecasters were abuzz over "the remnants of Hurricane Noel lashing the Massachusetts coastline and sending heavy rains inland." When we woke that Saturday morning, the sky was a heavy gray, and the rain started falling at around ten o'clock. Tim insisted he wanted to wait until afternoon and wouldn't mind running in the rain, and I didn't really mind the idea either. I told him that the hardest part of a run in the rain is the first five minutes. After five minutes, you are thoroughly soaked and know you won't get any wetter.

So we set out at about two-thirty in a soaking rain, just as predicted. Because I was fiddling with my new iPod, a birthday gift from Rick on my forty-first birthday the week before, I stepped in a big puddle on my very first step of the run.

Tim was so delighted with that turn of events that it carried us through the next two miles or so, just regaling ourselves with the memory of how Mom stepped in a *huge* puddle immediately and got *soaked*.

I complained about it far more than necessary because Tim seemed so amused by my complaints; he started threatening to change the name of our club from "We ain't no babies" to "We *are* babies," or "Mom equals baby; Tim equals not." His glee was making me laugh; the rain fell steadily; we were comfortable and happy for a very enjoyable, rain-soaked, 4.2-mile run.

Once November started, I began thinking about signing up for a road race with Tim. Racing has never appealed to me in the past, because I can't bear either the idea of driving an hour to go running, or the thought of paying for the privilege. But I've always loved the concept of a Thanksgiving Day race because it's such a nice offset to all that food, and the idea of having Tim do a race enticed me because it would be such an ego rush for him.

I went to CoolRunning.com to look for local options and discovered that there was one on Thanksgiving morning in Stow, only about ten miles from us. So I signed us up.

Tim's running log: Sun 11/4, 3 PM. Day 85. 5 miles. We set a new record!!

And then just as Tim was developing an interest in building mileage, Rick took the wind out of our sails by announcing that he thought we needed to back off a little. He was worried that Tim's skeletal system could suffer as a result of too much running, and he pointed out that when I asked the pediatrician about it, I said we were doing a mile a day; now Tim was talking about trying for a six-miler. Tim and I rolled our eyes, but of course I had to listen to Rick. I agreed that we could curtail the goal of logging a lot of miles during the week and keep weekday runs to the lower end of the one- to two-mile range. But maybe continue with longer weekend runs.

Rick's concerns notwithstanding, Tim and I set out to the Minuteman Bikeway and completed a five-miler. I couldn't remember the last time I'd run five miles, but it felt great.

Tim's running log: Tue 11/6, 6 PM. Day 87. 1.5 miles. My legs are still tired from Sunday.

One evening after the kids were in bed, Rick told me about a conversation he'd had while picking Tim up at school that day. He said that Tim's teacher stopped Rick on the school plaza at pick-up time to say he was disappointed with Tim's lack of motivation and occasional laziness.

Hearing this, I wanted to wail, "Noooo, anything but laziness!" since I'm convinced that intellectual laziness has been *my* personal bugaboo throughout my life. Out of my sisters, my seven first cousins and me, I'm the *only one* who does not have a postgraduate degree. I love reading, and discussing ideas, but I'm not intellectually ambitious the way all the other members of my extended family seem to be, and it is so important to me that my kids not inherit that particular trait.

I suspected Tim's teacher had mentioned it early in the year so that we could start working on it before it seemed like a bigger problem: well before conference time and report cards. I just hated the feeling that now I'd have to nag Tim more about school and we were going to start having homework problems; we were going to start developing negative feelings about school and schoolwork; we were going to start fighting over video games; all of it. Certainly there were worse things his teacher could report. I'd be more unhappy if he were bullying, or being bullied. But… laziness. It's like being overweight and convincing yourself you'll never let your kid overeat, and then hearing the pediatrician say, "He could stand to lose a few pounds."

Tim's running log: Fri 11/9, 6 AM. Day 90. 1.3 miles. At least it wasn't dark this morning.

When daylight saving ended, the sun rose a little earlier in the mornings, and Tim and I started running just after dawn again. Though he often awoke as cranky as a grizzly bear, Tim never protested that he wanted to go back sleep: he just wordlessly climbed out of bed, dressed for the run, and headed downstairs.

We were reaching the time of year when Tim always seems to become glum. Rick and I have long suspected that he might have Seasonal Affective Disorder, to some degree. The child simply seems to fade away along with the daylight. And it happens every year, as fall seeps into winter. He gets crabby and cranky and obstinate, but most of all, he gets *pallid*. He lies on our white couch as if he's going to transform himself into a piece of it.

Rick used to joke about actually getting rid of the couch just because we couldn't stand to see the way Tim clung to it during his melancholy moods. We liked the couch too much to let it go, but we sure did wish we could find a way past those melancholy moods.

I had hoped that our daily runs would stabilize his moodiness a little, but that didn't really seem to be happening in any measurable way. And yet he never hesitated to roll out of bed and lace up his running shoes when I told him it was time to go.

61

On a Sunday afternoon, we set out to do six miles on the Minuteman Bikeway. In the very last half-mile, I could sense Tim's discomfort. His throat was catching with little whimpering sounds, though not once did he make a motion to stop running. Nor was he out-and-out miserable. He was just pushing it. But it was the first run in many weeks that he didn't end by saying "Let's add on to that next week." Clearly six miles was his limit, and I didn't plan to test those limits again any time soon.

There are all kinds of reasons that kids Tim's age are interested in their bodies. At nine, he was still very much prepubescent, but I knew that as a growing kid, he would find his body and its changes of continuous interest. And the running presented a whole different way of viewing that. He was testing his body and finding out what it was capable of in terms of strength and endurance as it grew.

In that respect, he was at the opposite end of that spectrum from me. At forty-one, I was interested in seeing what I could *still* do. Six miles was routine for me twenty years ago, and for much of 2003 I did a weekly thirteen-mile run, but there was no denying the aging process. So while I tentatively explored what my body could still manage, Tim was discovering what his was just developing the ability to do.

CHAPTER 4

November 12 – December 12, 2007

After our six-mile run, it seemed for a while like we'd crossed a line. I worried that I had pushed Tim too hard. He seemed wan and weary, not just that day but for days to come. I started to think maybe all the naysayers on the CoolRunning.com message board were right, and he just didn't have the judgment to know whether this was a good idea or not.

On our three-month streak anniversary, Tim asked me if we could have another sundae celebration, like we did on the one-month anniversary. Even though I happened to know my mother had taken both kids out for ice cream that same afternoon, I acquiesced in honor of the milestone. After Holly went to bed, he and I headed to Friendly's. But just as we entered Bedford Center, he announced meekly that he didn't really feel like eating ice cream after all.

I asked if there was anything he *did* want, and there was: salt and vinegar potato chips from Whole Foods. So that was our celebratory food item: a bag of potato chips.

I talked to him about how maybe it was time to end the streak, and he did not demur. He did not really respond at all – but since normally he protested that idea vociferously, hearing him not respond was like a quiet concurrence. I pointed out we could still run together even without being on a streak. We could still do the Thanksgiving road race.

Rick gave me an iPod for my birthday at the end of October as well as a Nike Plus system, which plugged into the iPod to give us readouts on distance, mileage and speed as we run. Thinking it might work too as a motivator for Tim, I asked Rick to load the iPod with some music he thought Tim might like. I'm not much of a music person myself. When I have the radio on, it's always tuned to National Public Radio, and throughout high school and college I was always content to listen to whatever music my friends liked.

Rick's taste runs to classic rock, familiar tunes from the 70's and early 80's – our junior high and high school years – which I think of as Wayne's World music. But I agreed that Tim might like it. So Rick made Tim his own special playlist with all of Rick's old favorites: the Who, the J Geils Band, the Cars, Eric Clapton, the Rolling Stones, Aerosmith. Although I wasn't sure it was exactly how I wanted Tim's taste in music to lean, it was still amusing to hear him talking with Rick about the various bands. So along with running, Tim was getting introduced to classic rock.

By the middle of the week, Tim seemed to have bounced back. On that Wednesday evening, I picked the kids up at my parents' house and they were roughhousing wildly, so it was clear to me that he felt just fine physically. The six-mile run may have been a mistake, as Tim chose to remind me several times, but the streak remained intact, and I resolved to stick with shorter distances – three or four miles at the most.

I returned to the CoolRunning.com online discussion group to post a new question:

I just signed up for my first road race – a Thanksgiving day 5k. That's an easy distance for me and I'm not at all concerned about the running itself (nor do I have any hopes of posing any serious competition to anyone -- I'm just doing it for fun). My question is whether there's anything I should know about what it's actually like at the starting line of a race. I'm pre-registered -- how early should I arrive and what will be going on once I get there? What is the protocol around the starting line itself? Is there any special road race etiquette I might not be aware of? I do not know how many people will be there, but it's just a community event (it's not in my community, though, so I won't know people) -- but it won't be any big marathon crowd or anything like that. Thanks for the help.

Like the last time, replies poured in, but this turned out to be not nearly as inflammatory a subject as whether Tim and I should attempt a running streak.

I'd aim to arrive about 20-30 minutes before the race begins. You need to pick up your packet (race number, chip if any, shirt + other loot) and attach your number (and chip if used) and do whatever warm-up/stretching that you want. A half hour should be plenty of time. When you line up the basic idea is not to block anyone who's going to be much faster than you and you don't want to be blocked by someone much slower. There's a little bit of an art to figuring out where that is and the smaller the race the less it matters. Since you've said you're not "serious competition" I'm sure you'll be fine anywhere but the front line. If you're really not concerned with your finishing time then start in back and work your way up as you run (a good way to avoid the common mistake of going out too fast). You'll develop a sense for what place works for you after you've run a couple.

Race etiquette? Don't spit toward people you're passing. Pull off to the side to puke. That's about it. Seriously, I can tell you're a considerate person because you're asking two weeks before the race so just use your judgment.

Keep moving when you get to the finish line. Don't come to a dead stop because some people will be sprinting to the finish and you'll risk getting hit. Just move along and you'll be fine. Have a great race!

My first 5k they gave me a timing chip and being the dope I am I attached it to my bib instead of my shoe. Timing chips record only if they are on your foot. So when I crossed the finish line my time never calculated.

Have fun!!!

Make sure you go all the way to the finish line. It sounds like a no brainer, but I always see people stop before the finish line. Sometimes there are cones or something to guide you in, so maybe that tricks people up. The finish line is at the timing clock. Also, leave enough time for a trip to the porta-potty. There tend to be lines, and nerves may make you need to use it.

It helps to have someone along to pass off your t-shirt, goody bag, jacket, etc. to right before the start. If you don't have someone to bring along, give yourself time to run to the car right before the start (or find a place to hide your stuff). Look happy and victorious at the finish, no matter how you feel... you've gotta look good finishing. A personal one I have (and I think many people share) is not to wear the race shirt in the race. I like to earn mine before I wear it. Most importantly, make sure you have fun out there.

Pin all 4 corners of your bib onto your shirt. The first race I ran I just did the top 2 and it flapped the whole race. I usually bring a few small safety pins just in case the race doesn't have any (almost all do have them). On the back of your bib, jot down name and contact number of someone that can be reached in case of emergency. Double knot your shoe laces. If you have to stop for any reason (cramp, etc.), pull over to the side so you don't stop short in front of someone. Enjoy the race.

Thank the volunteers. A quick thank you to those at the water stop, those directing runners at turns, and those at the finish does wonders for those people not running, but are spending part of their Thanksgiving (or any race day) to make the event possible. Even if I don't get water at an aid station, I'll usually yell out something like "Thanks for coming out!" or "Thanks for the support" as I pass by.

If I haven't run the race before, I try to be there one hour early in case I get lost or have to find parking, etc. Don't sweat it, just have fun. Good luck.

Tim's running log: Thu 11/15, 6 AM. Day 96. 1.4 miles. Sun just coming up and kind of cold out.

I wasn't convinced that Tim was recovering from our six-mile attempt. And I was also beginning to see his irritability increase with the shorter days and diminishing daylight.

As the temperature dropped, I urged him to start wearing his fleece jacket, which had fit fine the year before but turned out to be a shade too small for him. I didn't see it as an insurmountable obstacle: to me it was obvious that he could surely deal with it until we had time to buy a larger one.

But the first time he wore it, he started getting crazy on the run, constantly tugging at the sleeves and neck in an exceedingly irritable and also sort of obsessive way. I so wanted him to just rise above it – *okay, look, once in a while your clothes don't fit comfortably; get past it* – but if there was one thing I'd learned in nine years – actually I learned this after about nine weeks – it was that you can't cajole Tim out of a bad mood.

My feeling was that we should push ahead to our one hundredth day and our Thanksgiving road race, and then reevaluate.

The *Globe* ran an essay I wrote about Holly and her imaginary friends. As so often happens, I wrote it with the fervent hope it would be published; I waited with bated breath to see it in the paper – and then the day it came out found me figuratively cringing under my desk awaiting the fallout. I never seem to think about the possible dangers until the article is in print, which speaks to how much I love appearing in print.

A part of me couldn't believe I wrote an essay about my hilarious and adorable five-year-old daughter and published it in the paper along with my name and hometown. *Interested in five-year-old girls? Come on by!* But then another part of me would say, *Look, you just can't be that paranoid; people looking for criminal behavior are not using the* Boston Globe's *essay segments to find it; and moreover, if the piece about Tim's athletic cup didn't bring pedophiles out of the woodwork, this one will not either.*

Boston Globe – November 15, 2007
My house is filled to rafters with 5-year-old's extended 'family'
By Nancy Shohet West

Our house is not small, but lately it's begun to feel crowded: There are the four generations of relatives, band members looking for practice space, and an au pair who spends hours jumping on the bed.

Not that I really have any right to complain. After all, they'd all be in the way a lot more if they actually existed.

In reality – and I use the term extremely loosely – the characters populating our household these days are my 5-year-old daughter Holly's cast of imaginary friends.

Other children might have an imaginary playmate or sibling; my child has an imaginary four-generation family that comes complete with a backstory worthy of a Danielle Steel novel.

But Holly handles her complicated world magnificently. In what she— and now my husband and I and our son – refers to as Pretend-Land, Holly is a 43-year-old mother of four. She has a husband, Ray, who comes from Africa and has multiple body piercings. The happy couple are parents to four children: three little ones and a daughter in her early 20s.

Why the age gap? Well, early in their marriage, right after the daughter was born, pretend-husband Ray did hard time – 10 years in the lockup for counterfeiting.

"He printed money off of money.com on his computer printer," Holly told me when she first explained Ray's sordid past. (There was little time for me to get to know my imaginary son-in-law during the couple's whirlwind courtship: They met at a pretend birthday party and were married three days later.) "Then he spent it. He didn't know you weren't allowed to do that."

Pretend-Ray's incarceration had an upside, though. He and his cellmates formed a band, and since their release from the Big House they've been quite successful. In fact, last month Ray quit his day job as a tow truck operator to devote himself full time to writing songs, recording in the studio, and performing.

As these responsibilities do not constitute a 9-to-5 commitment, he's also very hands-on with their three young children. This works out well because Pretend-Holly happens to be a small-business owner: She runs a "drink store," as Real-Holly explains it, which I assume is like a saloon, only with nonalcoholic beverages.

Balancing her role as a business owner with being a mom to three young children doesn't faze Pretend-Holly, because she not only gets a lot of help from Ray but also from the couple's adult daughter, Natalie. And luckily enough, a 20-year-old named Megan, who grew up in the same Pretend-Land neighborhood, recently offered her services as a live-in au pair because her own parents decided to move out of state and she wanted to stay near her friends. ("She doesn't have a boyfriend, but she wants to date Uncle Tim," Holly informed me. Real-Tim, Holly's brother and a typical 9-year-old boy, went through the roof when he heard this news.)

The most unusual thing about Pretend Au Pair Megan is that for exercise, she spends hours jumping on the bed every day. My pragmatic (and real) sister strongly recommended that I make sure Pretend-Holly is filing Pretend W-2s on the au pair, just in case there's a Pretend IRS.

It's only Real-Tim who occasionally reaches the end of his patience with our parallel universe – as happened a few days ago when Holly informed us that it was her son's birthday and she wanted to tell us what she was giving him for a present, but she'd have to whisper because he was *right there*. She whispered, and I couldn't hear her, so I asked her to repeat it, and she whispered louder, and I whispered back that I still couldn't hear.

"Mom!" Tim finally sputtered with righteous indignation. "Do you realize you're whispering so that a *pretend kid* won't hear you?"

Tim is right; there's no reason the rest of us need to immerse ourselves in Pretend-Land quite as thoroughly as we have. But recently I've started to think perhaps we can turn this into something a bit bigger.

I'm referring, of course, to the Hollywood writers' strike. Suddenly it seems that maybe there's a market for a 5-year-old who can spin out endless, mundane tales about an extended family and their quotidian routines.

Not that I would ever advocate crossing a picket line, but remember during the Major League Baseball strike several years ago, when the TV stations that had previously been airing Major League games started showing Little League tournaments?

Maybe there's room right now for a 5-year-old scriptwriter. Maybe it's time for Holly to meet Hollywood.

Of course, if we're really going to launch Holly into the entertainment world, she'll have the usual requirements of child stars. If she has to leave school to write scripts all day, she'll need an on-set tutor.

It can be a pretend one, though. Just don't tell the pretend Department of Education.

Tim's running log: Fri 11/16, 6 AM. Day 97. 1.5 miles. Short easy run.

Ever since we moved to the farm, I've considered mid-November my secret. It doesn't have the blazing foliage of October or the sweet soft greenness of June or even the picture-perfect snowy sparkle of winter. In mid-November, the fields are a burnished golden color and the sunlight shines through the bare trees. It is a season of magnificent earth tones. And I love the pre-holiday calm. Mid-November, to me, signifies light, peace, anticipation, the fact that there's still time to savor it all.

Tim's teacher wrote to me and said that although I might be somewhat right about the Seasonal Affective Disorder, he also thinks Tim doesn't like to be pushed to work hard. Discouraged as I was with that assessment, I also felt a little bit vindicated, like this teacher was seeing in Tim exactly what I had seen all along but had trouble getting anyone to concur with me about: he can be one tough nut to crack, with a shell that it's very hard to get through sometimes.

But a small part of me had really believed that this running program was therapy, that it would help exorcise some of Tim's minor demons. Tim's teacher was proving this not to be true, though: he had known Tim only *since* we started running, and he identified all the same behaviors I was trying to purge Tim of. So that made me feel like we weren't accomplishing much of anything at all.

Tim's running log: Sat 11/17, 3:30 PM. Day 98. 3.3 miles. Ran with John L. in New Hampshire.

We took a day trip up to southern New Hampshire to celebrate the birthday of the daughter of our good friends John and Anjali. Tim and I brought our running stuff with us because John likes running. They had already told the other guests about Tim's running streak, and Tim got lots of attention for it, which clearly pleased him. He usually clams up pretty fast around new people, but he was more than happy to talk about his running regime with them.

Once the party had died down a little, John took us out for a three-mile run around their neighborhood. Tim was happy to see a new route and to add a new guest – and a new state – to our runners' guest list.

Tim's running log: Mon 11/19, 6:10 AM. Day 100. 2 miles. We have now run ONE HUNDRED DAYS!!!!

On the morning of our one hundredth day of running, we were out the door just as the sun rose behind a medium scrim of clouds. Tim was ecstatic about the occasion of Day 100. To make it even more festive, he brought his beloved stuffed frog Ba along in his sweatshirt pocket. (Nothing says special celebration quite like an old stuffed frog.)

When we finished our first mile, we high-fived, since that officially made it Day 100 of running a mile, and then continued with the run; when we got home he whooped and hollered and updated the tally on the whiteboard himself, which for some reason he had never had any interest in doing before. Then he took a long, hot shower and dressed for school.

Tim's running log: Thu 11/22, 8:30 AM. Day 103. 3.1 miles. Our first road race: Stow Gobbler 5K.

On Thanksgiving morning, we left the house at 7 A.M. and got to the race with no trouble, even though it was several towns away in a region I did not know well. No sooner did we start walking across the parking lot than we saw our neighbor, who is a marathon runner and professional sports manager, and his teenage son. Since I did not expect to recognize a soul, it was such a coincidence, and such a meaningful one, to immediately see someone we knew and someone who even knew about Tim's running streak.

The route was along quiet, rural, car-free country roads, past some small rather run-down old places and some very spiffy new ones. The weather was perfect for running: thirty-nine degrees and misty, which seems to be ideal for getting the body moving. Every time I looked at Tim, he had a big grin on his face. Even though no one made a fuss over him whatsoever as a young runner, he just knew what he was doing was special and impressive, and he was so pleased with himself. He didn't need tons of external validation, which was a nice thing in itself.

Tim's journal
Nov. 27, 2007

"A half hour," says my mom.

"Okay," I say. It was Thanksgiving morning.

Time to get up. My mom woke me up. We got dressed, grabbed a bagel and climbed into the car. We are going to a 5K race (3.1 miles). When we arrived we went to the tent where we got our numbers (I was 273).

"Let's look at the map," my mom said.

We went over to the map.

Time to line up. We walk to the starting line.

BANG! We started running. About half a minute later it's not tight. We ran through a neighborhood, then the woods, then another neighborhood, next to a farm, and around a bend. Then we round a corner and come to a long road. At the end is the finish line! 0:33 after it started we crossed the finish line. Out of about 350 people I came in 115th place. "That was fun," my mom said.

We went to the drugstore and I got an Almond Joy. We got into the car and drove home.

I had not in any way anticipated that a secondary effect of streak running with Tim would be that it would make me start to feel old, or at least feel the effects of aging, for the first time in my forty-one years. I've always been astoundingly lucky in terms of health. Almost all of my family has. My father had cancer in his late fifties but survived, and one of my nieces had some pretty severe problems at birth that have in the years since been mostly resolved. Beyond those few things, we are incredibly blessed.

And not only am I fortunate in big ways regarding health: I'm just as lucky in small ways. If I run a fever once every two years, that's a lot for me. Same with stomach viruses. And perhaps most unusual, I never have running injuries. Admittedly, that could be because I'm a slow and short- to mid-distance runner; I don't necessarily do the kinds of things that often lead to injury, like intense training. But never a stress fracture, never a flare-up of any kind. It's something for which I feel amazingly fortunate.

But having said all that, as our running streak climbed past one hundred days, I had to admit to myself for the first time that I was feeling pretty middle-aged all of a sudden. In a word, creaky. After Thanksgiving the weather turned cold, and even though I didn't hurt anywhere, I felt like I'd lost the ability to build any momentum.

I had expected to be running for another twenty years. Actually, no: I'd never given a thought to how long I'd be running. I've always said that I believe walking is equally good exercise, and if I ever have to give up running for orthopedic reasons, I'd be fine with walking instead...but I never really pictured when and how that would happen. I hadn't thought of myself as aging, until I began to see how Tim's body was just starting to develop as a runner and it made me aware that maybe mine was just starting to corrode, though I certainly didn't feel corroded. I just felt...slow.

Thanksgiving vacation is the one time all year when I have enough time to get completely relaxed and no longer hurried, though it would be overstating the case to say it's when I get caught up. I always observe Buy-Nothing Day on the day after Thanksgiving; ideally I'd make it Drive-Nowhere Day as well, but that's always harder to pull off.

At the end of Thanksgiving weekend, I discovered that some college freshmen had been killed in a car crash the prior Wednesday, one of whom was the son of an employee at Town Hall. I didn't know the employee, and of course it shouldn't be any worse just because you find a connection with someone, but there's no doubt that it's connections that make you really start thinking about the awfulness of it.

I have long believed that Thanksgiving Eve is a date with a statistically significant number of serious car accidents, right up there with New Year's. My theory is strictly anecdotal; I've never seen any data to support this, but it seems to me that so many young people come home from college and immediately want to go see their hometown friends, so as a result there are a lot of very excited young people driving around in celebratory moods. My father lost a former student in this way, and five months before I met Rick, his roommate died in a Thanksgiving Eve accident. His name was Tim, and part of the reason we chose that name for our own child was in memory of him.

I just can't imagine how painful this must be. Raise a child for eighteen years, send him off to college, look forward to his coming home for a fall break and to start celebrating the holidays, and then that's it: his life just ended. How incredibly painful and awful for a family. To know that everything they were looking forward to is done now. To know today they'd planned to drive him back to school but now he won't be going back to school: his life is over.

I'd find myself looking at Tim and thinking, *How could I*

76

stand knowing I had only ten more years with him? It was just so awful to think about. And yet think about it is exactly what you have to do when something like this happens, so that you understand what it is to be empathetic and so that you appreciate all the times that awful things do *not* happen.

Tim's running log: Mon 11/26, 6 AM. Day 107. 1.4 miles. Cold and drizzly and up very early.

I talked to Tim about how "some people" – the anonymous participants on the online discussion board – thought it was a mistake for me to expect him to run every day. He responded with scorn, saying he runs every day because he wants to and it would be unkind of me *not* to let him.

I tended to agree with Tim. Their concerns were valid, but what it came down to was a mother's knowledge of her own son. Ultimately, I couldn't say that this was okay because his pediatrician said so or because Rick and I thought so or because Tim said he wants to do it; it was more that as his mother, the very core of my being carried an awareness of how he was feeling and what was okay for him, and I knew this to be okay.

None of the contributors to the message board knew Tim. I couldn't convince them; nor did I want to try. I could just fall back on that great cliché, mother's intuition, and feel certain that what he was doing was okay for him simply because I was his mother and I'd know if it wasn't.

As we ran early one morning in a light cold drizzle, Tim asked me, "Why is it that if you see a movie before you read the book, it ruins the book, but if you read a book before you see the movie, it doesn't ruin the movie?"

I turned it back on him, which is what moms usually do with questions like these, but in my case there was a hidden agenda: I often became too winded if I tried to talk a lot while running, whereas it didn't seem to affect Tim adversely at all.

"Why do *you* think that happens?" I asked.

He said he thought it was because you want to picture things yourself while you're reading, and not already know what it looks like. "Then when you go to the movie, you can compare it with what was in your mind's eye," he said.

I told him that the big exception to this principle for me was *The Devil Wears Prada*, because imagining all those fabulous outfits was simply beyond my realm of fantasy; I needed to see them on the screen in order to have any idea what they would look like. "Did you feel that way about the landscapes in *Lord of the Rings*? I asked him.

He said no. He didn't seem to think that anything at all was beyond the realm of what he could picture in his mind's eye.

Tim's running log: Tue 11/ 27, 6 AM. Day 108. 1.5 miles. We've been doing short distances this week.

Returning to work after Thanksgiving weekend, I had to acknowledge to myself, though not to anyone else, that I had the workplace blues. Corporate communications, at least in the life sciences, no longer seemed like a very good match for me. Some of the stories on my desk were so impenetrable and I was growing so frustrated with the fact that just because someone, somewhere, threw me the scrap of an idea, I had to run with it and make sense of it.

I felt like any admission I made of having trouble with this would be held against me, because anything negative I said became something to *work on*, something to improve, and therefore something to be judged by. If I said "I don't understand how to write about biomarker research and make it interesting," it would become my responsibility to *learn* about biomarker research and *make* it interesting, and if I couldn't, it became an example of something I neglected to do well.

Joan said, "Make the things you write here as interesting as what you write for the *Globe*," as if it were just a matter of approach or voice, but I choose my stories for the *Globe because* I think they'll be interesting. And in the rare cases where I am assigned a story, it's because an editor has already found some substance to it. Whereas what I was writing at work might well not *have* any substance; it might well just be that some manager at our Marietta plant saw his colleagues submitting stories and thought he'd better get cracking so as not to be bypassed by another business unit's accomplishments.

GUEST RUNNERS AND THEIR HOMETOWNS 11/30/07
John L. - Nashua, NH
Eric M. - Carlisle, MA
Nicole P. - Carlisle, MA
Austin P. - Carlisle, MA
Sophie R. - Swarthmore, PA
Alyssa A. - Sandwich, MA

DOGS
Angus P. - Carlisle, MA

STUFFED ANIMALS
Ba, a frog – Carlisle, MA

Tim's running log: Mon 12/3, 7 PM. Day 114. 1.5 miles. A lot colder than last week but I was fine.

December arrived hand in hand with winter weather. First the temperature dropped below freezing; then snow began to fall. I found myself moving like an old lady when we were out running: slowly, cautiously, ever afraid of falling.

Tim, on the other hand, bounded over the crusty snow cover like a gazelle, or like a jackrabbit. He actually resembled a rabbit somewhat, but he didn't know it: in the center of the back hem of his jacket was a triangle patch of reflective material. When we ran after dark, I'd wear our headlamp, and the light would reflect off the little triangle over his rump, making me think of the flash of white you see when a cottontail rabbit turns tail and flees into the bushes. I didn't share this with Tim but let myself be privately amused by it.

Tim's running log: Wed 12/5, 6:45 PM. Day 116. 1.5 miles. Fun to run in the snow!

As in past years, early December, with its short days and cold nights, found Tim frequently in a bad mood. At homework time, I'd go into his room just to keep him company while he scowled. One evening he dissolved into sobs over the issues of not having any pants he was willing to wear; hating not only his own winter coat but *all* winter coats; and not knowing what to write about in his journal for school.

What started it on that particular evening was Rick's declaration that Tim could not go another day wearing the same black sweat pants and red sweatshirt. Tim said he didn't have any other sweat pants he could wear, and Rick asked me why, and I had to explain that most of the ones I buy, Tim doesn't like; and when I find the kind he does like he outgrows them so fast.

But later that night, I had a revelation, which was that putting Seasonal Affective Disorder aside for the moment, Tim probably does suffer from mild obsessive-compulsive disorder. It made so much sense. His OCD didn't manifest as *doing* something – like washing hands – but rather about aversions, like to winter coats, clothes with buttons, any boxers other than the red-white-and-blue pair he wears to bed, and so on and so on.

This seemed coincidental, since the message board posters accused me of fostering OCD; but what I was seeing had nothing to do with the streak running. He just had obsessive tendencies as far as what he wouldn't do. But it was mild. And as I said to Rick, I wouldn't want to seek treatment because it was mild and it was just part of who Tim was.

After we reached the 100-day mark, I decided to devote my monthly *Mosquito* column to the streak. I've written essays about family life ever since the kids were born, and fortunately for me neither of them minds appearing in print. I asked Tim if it was okay with him if I wrote about our running endeavor, and he said it was fine. The glimmer in his eye suggested it was more than fine; he was excited at the idea of having our streak garner a little bit more attention.

But as I was drafting the column, I decided I should confirm with Ronald Kmiec that he didn't mind being cited as our inspiration. I emailed him, waited a day for a response, and then received a brief and startling note from his wife, Leslie, saying that Ronald was in the hospital, having suffered a heart attack over Thanksgiving, but that it was absolutely fine for me to mention him in my essay about Tim and me.

I wrote back immediately to express my concern, and didn't hear anything back, which concerned me. I knew that if he'd died I'd hear about it right away; in a small town, news travels fast. My concern was instead that he was having a very hard time coping with the end of his now more than 30-year streak.

I got my answer a week after my essay ran in the paper, not through a note from Ronald or Leslie but from the *Mosquito* itself, where Ronald had contributed his own essay.

Carlisle Mosquito
11,687 days: a streak comes to an end
by Ronald Kmiec

It was with a wistful smile that I read Nancy Shohet West's article about the running streak she started with her 9-year-old son, Tim, just as I was concluding my streak. I will be cheering Tim on to that 70-year goal!

The U.S. Running Streak Association considers *running at least one continuous mile within each calendar day under one's own body power for at least one year* as the minimum requirement for inclusion in their running streak listing. My first streak lasted from 4/19/74 to 11/16/75 (577 days) and was brought to an end due to an injury after two marathons and a 50-mile race in a 47-day period.

On November 28, 1975, after a two-week recovery period, I began what eventually would become the 14th longest consecutive day running streak in the U.S., extending over almost half of my life — 44,438 miles run over 11,687 days (3.8 miles/day) — one day short of 32 years. What started as an attempt to keep in shape, training for races, eventually evolved into a streak which developed a life of its own and became a defining aspect of my identity. I suppose most people would regard it as obsessive, and I'd have to agree with that assessment. I began to view it as the root source of my personal "fountain of youth," my sense of invincibility.

That confidence was shaken on Thanksgiving morning, November 22, 2007. I ran the Feaster Five race in Andover, along with thousands of other runners. Unexpectedly, I immediately felt an intense pain in the center of my chest, which persisted unabated for the first three miles, resulting in my slowest pace ever for a five-mile race, averaging 8:38/mile.

During the next few days, I still felt that something was "wrong," and my wife finally convinced me to see a doctor on the 26th for an exam and EKG. I was sent to the Emerson Hospital Emergency Room, where an extended battery of tests confirmed that I'd had a heart attack, resulting from a blockage in an artery. The following day, I was transferred from the Critical Care Unit to the Lahey Clinic. I underwent a coronary angioplasty, and a stent was inserted into one of the arteries supplying my heart on what would have marked the completion of the 32nd year of my running streak.

I now must await clearance from my cardiologist before I can resume running. The good news is that if I hadn't been such an "obsessive" runner and been in the shape I was, my doctor said I wouldn't be here today. I expected to be in the throes of depression when the streak ended, but am surprised that I have resigned myself to the current reality so easily. I was able to run through severe weather, illnesses, and injuries (meniscus tear, torn hamstring, fractured ankle, stress fracture, broken ribs) over the years, but the reality of a heart attack was the final wake-up call that forced me to call it quits.

To assuage my sense of loss, I still have four streaks remaining: the 34 consecutive Boston Marathon finishes, 32 consecutive five-mile and 26 one-mile Carlisle Road Race finishes, and my marriage of 33 years. I am grateful for the swift and excellent care I received, and am optimistic that I will be able to begin my next consecutive-day streak before the end of the year. And then, only 65 miles to go to complete my second circumnavigation of the earth at its equator (49,803 miles).

From: Nancy West
Date: 12/07/2007
To: Ronald Kmiec
Subject: Our thoughts are with you

Hi Ron,
I was relieved to read the update you published in the paper, as I was fearing the worst after hearing from Leslie last week. Mostly, I'm happy to hear that you are coping well with the sudden change in plans you've encountered! Tim and I will look forward to seeing you back out on the road soon, and we are hoping for your speedy recovery. It's so good to hear that your spirits are fine in any case. Hope you have a happy and healthy holiday season. Tim and I are at Day 117 and learning all about running in the snow and cold temps. The footpath has a few inches of crusty snow which for some reason I am having a lot more trouble dealing with than Tim is. I tell myself the reason I'm slower in these conditions is that he is half my weight and can bound effortlessly over it, whereas my feet keep sinking in. Surely it can't be a sign of age!
Best,
Nancy

From: Ronald Kmiec
Date: 12/08/2007
To: Nancy West
Subject: Re: Our thoughts are with you

Nancy,
Thanks for the email & kind thoughts. Perhaps when I get the go-ahead from my cardiologist we could coordinate the beginning of my next streak with a combined 1 mile run with Tim & you.
Ronald

Tim's running log: Tues 12/11, 6:30 AM. Day 122. 1.5 miles. A little icy but not that bad. Sun just starting to come up as we finish our run.

Mid-December brought the wintry weather I love: gray and overcast and raw, which is not the kind of weather anyone wants to see in March (when we often do) but perfect for the holiday season.

As we've done for the past three years on the second Sunday in December, Rick and I hosted the annual holiday party for our town newspaper, the *Mosquito*. All the board members and contributors along with their guests are invited, and it's one of my favorite holiday traditions. Everyone is always so appreciative of my efforts, and it's one of the rare times when I feel like the holiday ambience is perfect.

Not a minute went by in our house that I didn't feel thankful I still had it. I love the Christmas season because it is a yearly benchmark, and every year I'm just happy to be where I am: still alive, still with my family, still in our home, with the kids a year older and everyone still healthy and happy.

Tim's running log: Wed 12/12, 6 AM. Day 123. 2 miles. Air is cold but we are okay wearing a lot of layers of fleece.

CHAPTER 5

December 13, 2007 – January 12, 2008

Snow fell steadily throughout the month of December, which is not typical for Massachusetts. Not these days, anyway. Normally we might have one or two snowfalls around Thanksgiving and early December, but for the most part the weather tends to be dry or rainy, but not cold or snowy, through Christmas. The bulk of the snowfall in our region ordinarily happens in January and February. In winter of 2006/07, the first measurable snow fell on Valentine's Day, although by the end of the season the final numbers in terms of inches of snow were right up there with the average.

So it was a surprise that year, not so much that we had a snowy weekend in the very beginning of December, but that the snow that fell did not melt, and more snow continued to fall on top of it. The usual pattern of light snow followed by thawing or rain eluded us that year. Tim and I started running in the snow on December 3rd and didn't touch dry ground again for three months.

One reason I love the holiday season so much is that I feel like it's the one time of year when everything is just as it should be. For years, before we moved to the farm, I dreamed of the many ways I could create the perfect holiday celebration if only I had the right setting. Our ranch house near a shopping mall in Framingham just wasn't conducive to the ambience I wanted. If only we lived on a farm in the country, I'd be the Martha Stewart of Christmas celebrations, I believed.

Well, Martha Stewart I am not, but nonetheless, our holiday celebrations do tend to feel close to perfect to me. The farm setting is like a postcard; we have rituals and traditions, decorations and projects. It's the only time of year when I don't feel like I've fallen short of my potential. The weekend before Christmas, my sisters and their families usually arrive from their homes in Washington, D.C. and Pennsylvania. Once the younger children – Holly and Sarah's two – get caught up in the excitement, mild chaos often prevails, but for a while, with the house decorated and snow covering the ground, there's always the sense that we are having a holiday celebration worthy of a Christmas card scene.

For the previous several years I had been a hibernation runner, skipping the winter entirely. My credo was always that the running season ended when the temperature dipped below forty degrees. My favorite conditions for running are the end of a hot dry summer day as the sun starts to dip below the treeline, so that the air is warm but shade covers the roadway. I like running in as few clothes as possible: a tank top, shorts. But we had learned quickly how to counter the cold by layering on the fleece. And since we were out for only fifteen to twenty minutes at a time, it was easy, because we weren't running hard enough or long enough to overheat in those clothes.

But the ice presented a challenge for which I was not prepared. We slipped and slid all across the driveway. And the forecast predicted more precipitation and freezing temperatures. Ever the optimist, I said to Tim one day, "Okay, as a runner you've now dealt with heat, rain, cold, ice and snow. That pretty much covers the gamut."

On the phone, my sister Sarah asked me, "What are you going to do if Tim gets sick?" "Not go running," I said automatically. People were always asking me that, as if they expected me to say "We'll run even if he's sick."

No, of course we wouldn't. In a way, it was good for us that Ronald Kmiec's streak ended; it showed Tim that things happen and you deal. Unlike Ronald, Tim could easily enough stop and start again with every likelihood of breaking his past streak. Even with 124 days under our belts, it wouldn't take us all that long to get back to where we were.

Tim's running log: Fri 12/14, 6:30 PM. Day 125. 1.4 miles. Ten inches of snow fell yesterday. Easy to run on because it's been plowed.

I continued to struggle at work, feeling as if my manager had grown increasingly negative about my performance and I was being backed into a corner. I started thinking it might be a paradoxically positive thing to receive a bad annual review, so that I'd have something to feel righteous indignation over rather than having everything stay unspoken and under the surface.

For the first time, I started asking myself whether I would ever look for a new job. I had been genuinely happy at the biosciences company for my first year, and it seemed so unfortunate to me that things had gone south.

What I really wanted was for Rick's consulting business to begin doing well enough again that I could leave full-time work and just freelance. And that was a possibility and a dream, but definitely not close at hand in terms of reality. So I knew I'd just have to cope better with what I had.

Tim's running log: 12/15, 3 PM. Day 126. 2.4 miles. Cold but clear. Wore Dad's face mask and fleece gloves. Kept warm enough.

The following week, we woke to single-digit temperatures. By the time we ran in the evening, the mercury had risen to twenty degrees. As before though, the cold wasn't a problem, but the ice was. Tim tried running in his winter boots and found that it worked fine, so I started doing the same. It made for a heavy, clomping stride, but it was better than wiping out on the ice every few feet.

Other than for running, though, the weather was picture-perfect and beautiful. Stepping outside at ten-thirty for my nightly gaze at the sky, the air crystal clear and piles of sparkling white snow everywhere, I just had to say to the universe, *This is the most beautiful winter I have ever seen. I don't know whether you are giving us such a stunningly beautiful winter because for some of us it is our last, or maybe for all of us it is our last, but whatever the reason, it is breathtaking.*

So, Tim and I continued running and discovered that our bodies could take the cold, and we just hoped that the ice didn't do us in.

Tim's running log: Mon 12/17, 6 AM. Day 128. 1.4 miles. Cows were in the driveway because they don't like standing in the deep snow.

Giving more thought to why I was so unhappy at work, I realized that what I felt was *picked on.* For whatever reason, Joan was finding little ways to be unkind to me: cursory comments about my work, cold greetings, and then a strange decision one morning to command me to do errands, driving first to Staples and then to a Microsoft office, which was certainly not unreasonable but was just communicated in a very imperious way. So I started taking notes, jotting down examples of all the weirdness. I knew I'd made a few mistakes in stories I'd written, mistakes she had caught, like referring to a national conference as global; but I felt like she was somehow enjoying making a bigger deal of them than they were and using them to diminish me. *Picked on.*

Despite the issues at work, the build-up to Christmas continued to be something to savor. I baked every evening to make up gift baskets for the kids' teachers and a few of our friends: peppermint cookies, spiced nuts, cheese biscuits, fruit breads, and peanut brittle, chocolate truffles, eggnog cheesecake. I bought Dunkin' Donuts gift cards for the kids' bus drivers, and picked up stocking stuffers on random trips to the drugstore.

On the last day of work before Christmas week, Joan and I took a ninety-minute lunch at the Thai restaurant down the street from our office. We talked mostly about books and writing. I suspected that she was somewhat jealous of my journalistic success, but maybe that was just wishful thinking. Things were not particularly better around the office; we were on slightly warmer terms, but I continued to feel inept and overly watched.

Tim's running log: 12/19, 7:15 PM. Day 130. 1.4 miles. At the very end I slipped on the ice and fell right on my butt. IT HURT.

With more nights of baking, I remembered something random from last year: a line in a cooking article about finishing Christmas preparations early so that "while everyone else rushes around, you can put your feet up and wait for Rudolph." That image became my goal for the holiday season: staying ahead of the game enough so that on Christmas Eve, I had no work to do and could put my feet up, waiting for Rudolph. Or, more accurately, waiting to *become* Rudolph. But having a moment to put my feet up, in any case.

Tim's running log: 12/21, 7 PM. Day 132. 1.6 miles. Good pace considering the snow. Not as icy now so we were steadier even if not too fast.

On the Friday before Christmas, we had a holiday buffet luncheon at work and then everyone headed home. My goals for the afternoon were ambitious: pick out table favors, surprise Tim by being at the three o'clock school pickup, go to the post office to mail off the loaf of pumpkin bread I'd made for my aunt in Colorado, go grocery shopping, and fit in a run. Somehow I managed it all. With two weeks off from work a year, it was inexpressibly exciting to be on vacation. I still needed to get the house ready for guests – both of my sisters with their families would arrive in town within the next few days – and I still had tons of cooking to do. And there was that perennial pre-Christmas goal of getting ahead of the game enough that come Christmas Eve, I could put my feet up and wait for Rudolph.

At dinner that evening, the kids started bickering, and Rick and I read them the riot act as far as vacation behavior. I explained quite explicitly that a year is fifty-two weeks long and I had *two* weeks of those fifty-two as vacation, and I'd be damned if I'd waste one of my weeks listening to them quarrel. It was a pretty powerful argument, I had to say. I felt totally empowered afterwards. I'd stood up for my own right to have a good vacation, and I thought it made an impression.

Carlisle Mosquito – December 21, 2007
Santa under scrutiny
by Nancy Shohet West

Holly was sure she had it all figured out.

"Reindeer can't fly," she announced a few weeks ago. "So Santa isn't real."

"Santa isn't real?" I echoed, stalling for time. My son hadn't voiced this concept until he was eight years old; Holly is only five, and a rather young five at that, so I hadn't expected to be hit with it quite so soon.

"No, Santa isn't real," she declared with certainty, "just like mean people and monsters aren't real."

Wow. It was one of those where-to-begin moments. How unfortunate that she thinks

Santa isn't real; but great that she thinks monsters aren't real; and peculiar that she thinks mean people aren't real. Maybe it's worth sacrificing the Santa myth if it means retaining the latter two impressions.

"There's not really a Santa, but there are lots of adults who dress up like Santa and come to kids' houses in the middle of the night on Christmas Eve," Holly reasoned. It didn't seem quite fair to me that I was going to miss out on the fun of having a Santa-believer and at the same time be denied credit for gift-giving, but I figured if she wanted to see the world as full of furtive but benevolent adults sneaking presents into our home in the middle of the night, we'd let that go uncontested for the time being.

So many of the myths around Santa seem complicated when the cold hard reasoning of a five-year-old is applied. For years, we've hurried the kids off to bed on Christmas Eve, telling them it's crucial that no one see Santa. At some point one of them asked me why it's just fine for us to see him at the mall, at the town tree-lighting, at the church fair and the preschool potluck, but not on Christmas Eve. (At the church fair one year, we overheard Santa in a somewhat out-of-character discussion with the chair of the Finance Committee about the cost of necessary repairs to the church roof, which actually made perfect sense to my children. Who would have more of a vested Interest in the sturdiness of the roof than Santa?)

That was when I started to realize that Santa might have become a little overexposed. "It's just that he's in a hurry on Christmas Eve," I explained. "He doesn't want to see anyone because he doesn't have time to stop and chat." That explanation resonated quite well with my children, who are forever imploring me not to interrupt so many of our own public excursions with my propensity to stop and chat.

And then there's the obstacle we run into at church every year when adults try to explain why we all get together to fill stockings for underprivileged children in a nearby city. "Think of all the presents you get on Christmas. And imagine: If it wasn't for us, these other children might not receive anything at all!" one well-meaning adult exclaimed merrily last year to a Sunday school class. This left the kids at our church with the befuddling message that Santa takes good care of wealthy children while completely ignoring the less fortunate.

But what surprised me more than Holly's Santa insight this year was that she seemed to have forgotten it just days later. "Mom, there's something I've been thinking about," she said with a very worried look. "What happens if I need you in the middle of the night, and it's while Santa is here? What if I need to go to the bathroom and I call out for you and Santa hears? Won't he leave if he thinks someone is awake?"

I was tempted to use her anxiety to my own advantage by suggesting that at the age of five, maybe she could learn to use the bathroom during the night without waking me up first.

"Santa will be downstairs and we'll be upstairs," I said. "He won't care if we're up, as long as we don't try to catch a peek at him."

"But what do kids do if they need their moms and their bedrooms are on different floors?" Holly continued. This was the same kid who had announced days earlier that Santa wasn't real. But I guess worries about pee accidents trump holiday myth revelations. "Just come get me like you always do," I sighed.

I'm sure that with time, reality will encroach, so for now we'll enjoy a final season of quasi-belief for our household. And if Holly's uncertainty about Santa's presence means that she'll use the bathroom without waking me on Christmas Eve, we'll just call it our Christmas bonus.

Tim's running log: 12/22, 4:30 PM. Day 133. 1.4 miles. I was really really tired before we even started.

I found myself dwelling on how even though mentally I loved running more than ever as Tim and I built up our streak, I was feeling increasingly less physically able to perform. This continued to surprise me – the indication of aging, just after my forty-first birthday.

A year earlier I had read a memoir written by Darcy Wakefield as her body was gradually breaking down from multiple sclerosis. She described a very specific fantasy of what death would be like: upon dying, she would find herself on a beach, with miles of rolling surf and packed sand…and God would walk up to her and hand Darcy her favorite pair of running shoes.

Running is such a wonderfully physically liberating thing, and anything that makes you feel like you're getting worse at it can be profoundly disturbing because it's a sign of mortality. I loved running with Tim; someday, I knew, I would no longer be running with Tim at all; and someday I wouldn't even be on this earth with Tim anymore. True no matter what, but somehow particularly clear in relation to running.

Tim's running log: 12/23, 3 PM. Day 134. 3.5 miles. My uncle John ran with us because he is visiting from Washington D.C.

I woke up on Christmas Eve day with a couplet in my head:

> *Twas the day before Christmas,*
> *not yet eight o'clock*
> *And the cousins were already*
> *starting to rock.*

If they weren't exactly rocking, they were at least having fun so far: playing and chattering and not yet fighting, though I knew that quarrels would break out before the day ended. Holly and my sister's daughter Hannah, who were just ten weeks apart in age, still couldn't play together for more than twenty minutes without a fight erupting, it seemed.

This is something I've learned about being a parent to young children: you should give up all dreams of the picture-perfect Christmas. Oh, the ink I've expended writing about how hard it is to make the holidays go smoothly just when you most want them to, when your kids are small. I can never suppress a snort when anyone talks about how "Christmas is for children" or "the magical experience of a childhood Christmas." True, preschoolers can get that mesmerized look in their eyes when they gaze at a Christmas tree or a shopping mall Santa Claus, but in my experience, Christmas is actually really hard with young children, because they get so overexcited and they fall apart so easily. So I've learned not to have high hopes for how magical it will be and just try to keep everyone on an even keel emotionally. Little kids at

96

the holidays make for great photo ops, but not necessarily the happiest of memories.

On the 24th, I cooked all morning. Our tradition since moving to our Carlisle house has been to go to the three o'clock family service at church and then host my family for a Christmas Eve dinner of homemade pizza. For me, walking to church is part of the mystique of the day, but this particular year it just wasn't practical: with the snow banks as high as they were and the footpaths unplowed, we would have been walking in the road. So I put aside romantic notions of a brisk Christmas Eve afternoon walk and we drove to church instead.

Back home, I bustled around to get our Christmas Eve dinner ready. I thought I was ahead of the game, but as is inevitable on Christmas Eve, things started deteriorating by about five o'clock. Holly and Hannah seemed to have equally spaced intervals of playing happily and skirmishing, and I was embarrassed by what a bad host Holly was being: bossy and demanding and repeatedly bursting into tears. I expect her to manage better than that even at the age of five.

"It's like a hockey game around here," I muttered at one point in regard to the little fights that kept breaking out. Finally my sister Lauren's daughters drifted over from my parents' house. Phoebe offered to oversee a sledding excursion on the hill in our yard, which was a lifesaver, and Sophie sat at the kitchen counter to visit with me while I cooked. Getting the younger kids outside made everything better, for them and for me alike.

A new song called "Christmas in Fallujah" by Billy Joel had been playing on the radio all month, and every time I heard it, I was reminded of how many awful and heartbreaking ways there are to spend Christmas: as a soldier in a dangerous situation unable to go home, or as someone who is at home but can't afford to turn on the heat Christmas Day let alone buy presents, and so on. As I prepared dinner, I started thinking about all the ways to finish the sentence "This is the first Christmas since." Since I lost my husband, since the diagnosis, since the divorce, since the breakup, since the baby was born, since I lost my job, since we got married, since we moved into our own home, since we lost our home. Christmas is such an emotionally loaded time, which makes it poignant and beautiful and difficult all together.

Tim's running log: 12/25, 5:30 PM. Day 136. 1.5 miles. Very dark and VERY icy. My mom was more scared than I was.

When I was growing up, we spent Christmases with my grandparents in Colorado. After breakfast, we usually walked a mile up the road to my cousins' house, and often we went skiing later in the afternoon. So staying indoors for all of Christmas Day, which tends to be what happens with my current family configuration, bothers me. And for weeks, I'd been dreaming about a long, exhilarating Christmas Day run.

Tim and I did in fact have a memorable Christmas run, but not for the reasons I wanted: not because it was long and exhilarating but because the ice made it so harrowing. We didn't get back from visiting Rick's family until after dark, and the ice on the driveway was so thick and slippery that I was terrified and miserable the whole time.

We eked out a little over a mile by running to each of the houses on the common driveway and then out to the road, and at one point on that very minor slope (so minor, in fact, as to be imperceptible in normal conditions) near the neighbors' barn, I found myself sort of stranded, jogging in place on a rough snowy spot surrounded by slick ice and afraid to move.

"C'mon, Mom, it's not so bad!" laughed Tim, the mountain goat, who seemed unaffected by the ice as usual. Finally, I trudged onward. We made sure we were always moving at no less than a light jog, so it counted as running, but never had I run so slowly or cautiously. Not the wondrous Christmas Day run I'd hoped for at all, but at least we got out there.

Tim's running log: 12/26, 2 PM. Day 137. 2.1 miles. We went out to the main road just to get away from the ice.

Boxing Day has always been one of my weird and secret pleasures, and I'm a little surprised more Americans don't observe this traditional British holiday on December 26th. Seeing the words printed on the *National Geographic* photo calendar when I was young always made me picture fighters with big red boxing gloves held in front of their faces, but eventually I learned that it was the day when wealthy land owners would box up leftovers for the serfs – hence the "boxing" terminology.

As a kid, I loved the day after Christmas because it meant I could play with all my new toys; in college, it meant the holiday rush was over and I still had two weeks to go before returning to school: time at last to sleep and watch movies and catch up with my high school friends.

As a parent, I love Boxing Day because it is the one day of the year when my kids are self-sufficient in terms of recreation. All they want to do is rummage through their new gifts; they never need a thing from me. I don't have to cook because we always have so many leftovers. So I usually spend Boxing Day sorting through the kids' toys and whatever we've received; cleaning up the Christmas Day mess; and when possible gathering armfuls of old, outgrown toys that I can secret into boxes and eventually on to Goodwill without the kids noticing, now that they have so much new stuff.

I know several families who continue their Christmas festivities into the 26th, with still more relatives to see and more gifts to exchange. When the day after Christmas dawns, I'm always so suffused with relief about not having to be anywhere or get the kids bundled up to go anywhere that I can't imagine choosing to do that. As I said to Holly, Boxing Day is a great day to be at home, put away your new things, take a long bath, play some new games, not have any plans. All I wanted to do was fit in a run, organize an afternoon game of Scrabble, and help Holly learn to hold her new guitar.

Sarah's family was packing up to leave: John's siblings

were waiting for them in Tennessee. I hoped that the get-togethers would get easier as the kids got older. Although I was so happy they'd visited and stayed with us, it was draining to keep monitoring the kids' behavior. I took full blame on Holly's behalf; she was the instigator, but it was just exhausting. At the age of nine, Tim was finally at the point where Christmas-related meltdowns were not really even imaginable. Small children are wonderful, but there's just no question that life gets easier as they grow.

Tim's running log: 12/27, 3 PM. Day 138. 1.5 miles. We drove to the Center and ran on Church Street. Wet snow falling but the pavement was dry and not slippery.

Most families I know leave their Christmas decorations up through New Year's Day, but we always un-decorate a few days after Christmas. Mostly, this is because Rick starts worrying around that time that the tree is drying out and presenting a fire hazard, and once we put away all the tree ornaments, it just makes sense to keep going. In early December, when we first take out all of our holiday decorations, I always worry that it will be depressing to put everything away again afterwards, but when the time comes, I find it cathartic. The house always seems so beautifully sparse and clean once all the holiday knick-knacks have been cleared away. It's a job I'm happy to do by myself, removing each delicate item from its place one at a time.

Packing Christmas decorations is always a little bit wistful. Not sad, as I am not one to mourn the end of the holiday season; but a little uncertain. It makes me think about time passing: how each of these ornaments and knick-knacks is something I will not touch again for another fifty weeks. Almost a whole year will go by before I see these items again, and what will I know then that I don't know now? What secrets does the upcoming year hold that I'll be amazed when next December comes around to realize I had no inkling of as I stood here putting away the ornaments?

Waking on the morning of New Year's Eve, there were two things on my mind. The first was how much I was dreading the return to work after January 1. I knew I needed to focus on improving my work performance and getting along better with Joan. Despite the anxiety, I kept reminding myself of how I felt two years ago when I was so desperate to find a job; I couldn't have imagined complaining about work then, and the fact remained that I had such a *good* job. If only I could apply myself better to it.

The other topic on my mind was how well 2007 had turned out, overall. I'd had so many articles published, we held on to our house, we were still financially afloat (though gasping for air), and we all got along well and had fun together. And the kids were doing so well.

What I really wished for in 2008, besides an absence of terrorist attacks on a global level and serious illness or injury to my personal circles, was some flicker of hope that I could leave full-time work soon. I was really tired of working forty hours a week, even at a great job. I wanted to be at home, to be available to the kids, and to work harder on my freelance projects. That was what I really wanted to be doing. So, shallow as it sounded in comparison to the absence of terrorist attacks, a hope for the new year or maybe the next one was to come closer to a point where that might happen.

I take New Year's resolutions very seriously, in part because I tend to be relatively successful at reaching them. Or maybe I have that backwards; maybe I tend to succeed at my resolutions because I take them seriously.

My foremost resolution for 2008 involved punctuality. I wanted to learn and implement strategies for being on time all the time, not just very occasionally. I wanted to make punctuality a new part of my inner appearance, the way a new haircut might become part of an outer appearance. I wanted people to say, "Wow, look at you – you're on time to places now!" I wanted to make it part of who I am.

And another old favorite: get more sleep. Stop counting on the adrenaline factor to get you up in the morning. Be in bed by ten o'clock. Skip some of those evening chores if you need to. Be someone who makes it a priority to get a good night's sleep every night, even if it means letting laundry go unfolded once in a while. Sleep matters, and there's no way to make up for it.

GUEST RUNNERS AND THEIR HOMETOWNS 12/31/07
John M. - Washington, DC
John L. - Nashua, NH
Eric M. - Carlisle, MA
Nicole P. - Carlisle, MA
Austin P. - Carlisle, MA
Sophie R. - Swarthmore, PA
Alyssa A. - Sandwich, MA

DOGS
Angus P. - Carlisle, MA

STUFFED ANIMALS
Ba, a frog – Carlisle, MA

Tim's running log: 1/1, 2 PM. Day 143. 1.1 miles. Snow fell all day so we ran on the driveway right after it got plowed.

While we were out running in the freshly plowed snow on New Year's Day, we noticed that our neighbors had a Dennis Kucinich bumper sticker on their car. Tim asked me who that was, and I explained he was a presidential candidate, then commented (probably incorrectly – I am surely the most politically uninformed person in Massachusetts) that Kucinich, as a relatively young, bright, popular, middle-of-the-pack candidate, was the type who would probably drop out soon but might very well resurface as a vice presidential candidate.

Tim asked me what the difference between president and vice president was, so I explained the role but also the crucial importance of "one heartbeat away." Of course, once I said that the vice president becomes president if the president dies or gets fired, he wanted to know what a president could get fired for and whether that's ever happened...causing me to try to explain Watergate.

It was a laughably lame explanation: "The president's team broke into a hotel room to get private information, and he was generally very dishonest..."

So why didn't he go to jail rather than just lose his job, Tim wanted to know?

Happily, I restrained myself from bringing up the impeachment and near-firing of President Clinton, which I actually could have explained far better than Watergate. I'd like to think that's simply because I was a cognizant, news-reading adult during Clinton's tenure and not because it's just easier for me to explain extramarital affairs than government secrets.

Tim's running log: 1/4, 6:15 PM. Day 146. 1.4 miles. So cold my face and eyes and everything else hurt.

With the coldest weather of the winter kicking in just after New Year's, Tim and I stopped trying for morning running: I just didn't even want to go through the farce – or the time-waster – of trying to wake him. One evening as we headed out, the temperature was fourteen degrees and the wind chill was unbelievable. It was the kind of weather where you moan in misery when the wind blows. I did have a passing concern that I might be subjecting Tim to frostbite, but I was fairly sure frostbite involved a longer duration of exposure than this was.

Carlisle Mosquito – January 4, 2008
I'm late, I'm late — but not in 2008
by Nancy Shohet West

I read an article about New Year's resolutions recently that gave this pointer: to increase your odds of succeeding with a resolution, tell it to as many people as possible. So, what better way to ensure the success of my own 2008 goal than to put it forth to 5,000 people — many of whom will be able to personally monitor my progress in the upcoming months? (If you doubt that the readership of the *Mosquito* is actually 5,000 — birds in cages looking down from their perches not withstanding — note that I forward my column to a *lot* of friends and acquaintances every month. And "becoming less self-promotional in 2008" was decidedly not one of my resolutions. Maybe in 2009.)

Thus, here it is: My resolution for 2008 is to overcome a lifetime of being chronologically challenged. Or, to put it more bluntly, late to everything.

I know I'm not alone in saying it seems that the past several years have gone by in a blur, but in my case I mean it literally: a blur because I've spent so much time rushing. I arrive at work late, get to meetings late, reach social events late. I leave the house late when I'm supposed to be somewhere, and I leave late from wherever I am when I'm supposed to be home. I miss the announcements at church and the previews at movies. Anyone who is a frequent dinner guest at our house knows that it's not at all unusual to pass me out on a run as they turn into our driveway.

My husband does not have this fault at all, and I always tell myself if I only follow his example, my problem will be instantly solved. He's always on time. And yet whenever we're going any place together, I argue with him about what time to leave and manage to stall until we're on my schedule rather than his.

Every now and then, I have the surprising experience of getting somewhere early, and it always feels so wonderfully refreshing that I wonder why I don't do it more often. I inexplicably arrived at a parent-teacher conference ten minutes ahead of schedule last month — something I haven't done in the past three years of parent-teacher conferences — and not only was able to examine the bulletin board displays in the hall, which had previously just been a blur of bright colors to me as I flew by — but also had the chance to chat with a passing staff member whom I hadn't seen in a long time.

Turning myself into a punctual person would mean eliminating the physical stress of always running behind schedule: the fast heart rate and stress headache I get from watching the minutes tick by. And, of course, there are always after-effects of arriving late: weathering the resentment of those who arrived on time; fumbling for pens at a meeting when everyone else already has theirs out; missing the instructions. Or worse. With my two children and one niece in tow, I once arrived ten minutes late for a long-scheduled family portrait. The kids were so stressed out by all the rushing that they were unable to sit and pose for the photographer. As other family members were quick to point out, I ruined the plan for everyone, simply by not admitting that it can easily take up to ten minutes to get three kids from the playground across the parking lot and into the car.

But a few weeks ago, I had a breakthrough of sorts. My children and I were going to visit relatives who live nearly an hour away. We hadn't visited them in well over a year, but what I remembered most about arriving at their house in the past was that they always teased me about my lateness. This time, I decided, I simply didn't want to make that the premier topic of conversation. If for no other reason than to ensure that we'd have to find something more interesting to talk about, I resolved to be on time just to cut off that conversational avenue.

So I left my house fifteen minutes early. It worked. And I realized that if I could do it that once, surely I could do it again.

I once attended a lecture on personal organization at which the instructor observed, "Any time you get something you want, no matter how much you wanted it, there is something you will sacrifice." In my case, if I start making it a high priority to be on time, I'll lose all those little three- or five- or fifteen-minute pockets of getting one last thing done at home before I leave the house. But it's probably worth a try anyway. I can always go back, and make a resolution *next* year to stop wasting so much time by arriving places early.

It's highly unlikely I'll reach that point. But the idea of being able to change something negative about myself is so intriguing. Can I become a different kind of person, someone who is serene and organized and completely centered at every gathering or event? Unlikely. But at the very least, I can set the stage to try to make that a possibility.

Tim's running log: 1/5, 3 PM. Day 147. 2.7 miles. Ran with Nathan in their neighborhood.

Most of the features I write for the *Boston Globe* are my idea; I come up with a story angle and pitch it to my editor, who tells me whether he thinks it's worth pursuing. Every now and then, he gets creative and suggests a story idea to me. Early in January, he asked me to do a story on local sledding hills.

"I bet I'll dig up a lot of controversy on that topic," I muttered to myself. What was there to say about sledding? It's fun; kids love it; it's a great way to be outside in the winter. That's an article? Worthy of the *Boston Globe*?

But when my editor gives me an assignment, I do it. So off I went on a Saturday morning to research sledding, starting at a public park in a nearby town.

When I arrived at the hill, there were about thirty people of all ages sliding down the slope. What really struck me was how much fun they were all having: All these parents out sledding with their toddlers and preschoolers were so elated with the conditions and the general situation.

And although this wasn't why I was there, I couldn't help feeling both envious and guilty that they seem to know how to have fun with their kids better than I did; I felt like what they were doing was something I never do, or at least wasn't doing at that moment: just going out and having a blast.

And then I drove on to another public sledding area in another town and found just one group sledding on that hill: a woman named Kristen with her daughter and her daughter's friend, both about Tim's age, and I couldn't get over how happy this woman seemed. It was as if she honestly couldn't imagine anything more great than being out sledding.

On the way home I kept thinking about her and wondering: *Doesn't she have housework to do? Cooking for the rest of the week? Did she bring any work home from the office? Is her house all picked up from Christmas? Doesn't she have any errands she needs to get done? How is it that she's so happy to be out sledding?*

107

I felt like she had a secret that I wanted in on: how to be so happy and have so much fun on a Saturday morning. I wanted to follow Kristen home and find out what the rest of her life was like and how she makes a Saturday so much fun, when for me, it's just a relief when my kids find things to do around the house so that I can get other things done.

Tim's running log: 1/7, 6 PM. Day 149. 1.4 miles. We talked about the candidates for president.

Mostly just to initiate a conversation while we ran, I remembered that Tim watched some of the candidates' debate so I asked him what he thought of it. He told me he'd support Barack Obama for president. I asked why, wondering if it might be based on nothing more than appearances or gender allegiance.

Tim surprised me: he said, "He has a lot of good ideas for education. He said we're twenty-seventh in the world for math and science and he wants to improve that. He also wants to end the war in Iraq. I think he would work on the right things."

Tim's running log: 1/8, 7 PM. Day 150. 1.6 miles. WARM OUT!!! We are having a January thaw!!!

Shortly after the coldest weather of the season, we had a January thaw. The temperature rose into the sixties, and a significant amount of ice melted off the driveway.

Tim was exuberant; in fact he was *giddy*. He tore off his sweatshirt after about ten minutes and hooted, "I'm running in a t-shirt! I'm running on ice in a t-shirt!" Yes, it was still icy in places, and slippery with water coating the ice, but Tim's ecstatic bearing made me laugh.

I was being careful because of the ice, and Tim was jabbering away because he was so excited about the weather, and at one point he said "Mom, this is *exactly* the opposite of usual: I'm chatting and you're hardly saying anything."

Tim didn't grasp at all that this was a January thaw and wouldn't last; he was convinced spring had arrived. "I *knew* this would happen," he announced smugly. "Winter started early and it's ending early."

Since there have been so many times over the years when I too became seduced by balmy weather in the middle of winter, I knew exactly how he felt. A week ago, I pointed out to Tim, we had a snowstorm, followed by single-digit temperatures. This wouldn't last either. But it certainly was fun.

Tim's running log: 1/11, 6 AM. Day 153. 1.2 miles. Looked like rain falling but it was really an icy glaze in a steady rainfall. Pretty unpleasant! But we did it!

Martin Luther King Day weekend marked the fourth time I attended an annual women's retreat in Connecticut with about twenty women from my church. I found out when I got home that Tim headed out on Saturday afternoon and did about 1.3 miles going from house to house on the driveway. He said he didn't enjoy running alone all that much, but it didn't seem to occur to him to skip it.

For my part, I luxuriated in a solo run, my first one in months. I ran for five miles along wide paved roads in the farmlands of northeastern Connecticut. It was good to be out pushing myself although it was not one of those runs where I reached a point of feeling ecstatic or effortless. But I kept thinking about how for the rest of the day, I'd remember it as a great run, how the sense of absolute well-being would settle in as soon as the run was over, and even more so once I'd taken a shower and put on warm dry clothes.

And, inevitably, then I started thinking about allegories of parenting. There are so many times when you watch yourself and you know you're doing a good thing and should be feeling great, but you're really just too conscious of how much effort you're putting forth to really enjoy it. I often feel that way over the holidays: *this should be it, this should be absolutely joy, this should be the ideal, but I still have a dessert to make and I hope Holly and Hannah don't start fighting again and what time am I going running?*

But then afterwards, you just think about how great it was simply because you succeeded. I look back on Tim's babyhood and think, okay, it was a little challenging, but I must have been enjoying the sense that I was doing a good job. Same with running: wow, I ran five and a half comfortable miles; that must have been a great run. Well, yes. It was. But it's also great to look back on once it's over.

Tim's running log: 1/12, 11 AM. Day 154. 1.3 miles. Mom is away so I ran by myself out to the road, over to the neighbors' house, and back.

CHAPTER 6

January 13 – February 12, 2008

The winter of 2008 wore on and on and on. Snow fell; ice accumulated; frigid temperatures prevailed. Tim and I ran on, despite the fact that every time I left my office on a pitch-dark, frigid weeknight at five-fifteen, I'd look across the parking lot and think, "I can't do it. I can't go home just to change into running clothes and head out on foot. I'm tired of this."

We persevered. We slipped and slid. We wondered why we'd started this arcane challenge, at least I did. Tim never questioned it; he seemed further invigorated as it got more and more difficult to negotiate the terrain.

Tim's running log: 1/14, 4:30 PM. Day 156. 1.3 miles. Snow fell all day and we didn't have school. Mom stayed home from work too. We went running after the driveway got plowed. Pretty slippery but also kind of fun.

I kept thinking of the infamous "Master of My Domain" *Seinfeld* episode, in which Kramer, knowing that he has lost the challenge, walks into Jerry's kitchen, slaps down a $20 bill on the counter and says "I'm out." I kept fantasizing about slapping a bill – of any size, or not even a bill, maybe a half-frozen wool glove – on the table in front of Tim and saying "I'm out."

One thought that pushed me along, though, was that Tim and I were continuing to receive a lot of credit from people who knew about our undertaking – credit we would not have gotten had it been another one of our recently typical mild winters. If it was a year more like the previous year, with little snowfall, everyone would say to us "Oh *sure* you can run every day...*this* winter! You haven't had to face any *real* winter weather!" No one could voice doubts that this year we were contending with a true New England winter.

Tim's running log: 1/15, 7 PM. Day 157. 1.2 miles. Cold and icy so we did a short run. Talked about bands I like.

Psychologically, the winter was taking its toll on me. It wasn't even the cold; it was the darkness. The snow cover meant that we couldn't run along the main road, only along our long common driveway, and it was getting boring, boring, boring. I just kept reminding myself that dark icy snowy winter nights would surely be the hardest part of the year as far as running, and unless Tim or I got very sick or injured, it surely wouldn't get any harder than this, only easier.

In a fit of late-January cabin fever, I looked up April road races. What I really wanted was a 5-miler, less than a 30-minute drive from home, with an entry fee that added up to no more than forty dollars for the two of us.

We were planning to travel to Pennsylvania to see my sister Lauren's family on Patriots' Day weekend, as we'd done the year before. Patriots' Day, a New England holiday commemorating the start of the Revolutionary War – whose iconic moment was the battle fought at the Old North Bridge, where Tim and I did our first 3-mile run back in November – is one of the few Monday holidays my company observes. The extra day off gives us enough time to fit in the long drive; and it comes at the beginning of the kids' school vacation week, so it makes them feel like they'd done something special for their vacation even if I then have to go back to work for the remaining four days of the week.

To my great luck, I found a race listed the very same weekend we planned to visit in Valley Forge, Pennsylvania, and when I e-mailed Lauren about it, she said that was just forty-five minutes from where they live. Tim seemed excited about the idea, and I was encouraged to think maybe that would inspire us to build up our mileage a bit once we drew closer to winter's end.

1/21, 6:45 PM. Day 163. 1.4 miles. Temperatures still low but we bundled up in fleece and felt fine.

Time management is always a challenge for me; that winter it seemed to be more problematic than ever. After one run on an evening that was so cold we both wore face masks, I found myself inordinately annoyed by the sensation that my makeup was rubbing off all over the mask.

I could have just taken the time to wash my face before we headed out running, but in fact that was exactly the problem – I couldn't. I felt like I did not have one second to spare in the evening after work. As soon as I arrived home each evening, Holly wanted to cuddle and chat and be close together (following me into the closet, into the bathroom, in and out of my home office as I turned on my computer); I'd get dinner started, change my clothes, get dinner on the table; we'd eat; I'd start Holly's bath; and then Tim and I would head out. Not one second in there to spare.

And it was the same after our run: I'd read to Holly, put her to bed, play Scrabble with Tim, put him to bed, make lunches and snacks for the kids' school day, write notes about dismissal plans for school, prep coffee for the morning, and mix up a marinade for the next night's dinner. And then it was ten o'clock and time to go to bed – but first I needed to fold some laundry and write a check for Holly's book order. No time to wash my face before ten-thirty. Even though it only takes, what, two minutes?

This was how all mothers of young children felt, I realized, whether they were in an office from eight-thirty to five as I was or based at home all day. So... there it is. My makeup gooked up my face mask because my days were just too full for me to take the time to wash it off.

113

My friend Marilyn, who is the features editor for the *Mosquito*, asked if she could use my jog stroller when her new grandchild visited from Pennsylvania. I realized that I could not only let her use it; I could give it to her permanently. With my youngest child five years old, I didn't need it anymore.

I spent a morning trying to clean it up from its nine years of hard use, and it was a very strange feeling. More than anything else we've given up post-baby, that felt like the end of an era to me. I'd had that stroller since Mother's Day of 1999, so eight and a half years, which sounded like an underrepresentation given how much mileage it had accrued.

Dozens of runs through our Framingham neighborhood when Tim was a baby. Then after we moved back to Carlisle, walks with Tim up to the library or church. The spring after Holly was born when I first put her in the stroller and went for a 40-minute run, ecstatic to be out running again. When Tim started kindergarten, I'd put Holly in the jog stroller every morning so that we could walk him to school, except most of the time he ended up cadging a ride on the footrest for at least part of it. And the previous summer, though normally I might have said a five-year-old was too old to ride in a stroller, it gave Tim and me the option of taking Holly along for a run.

So folding it up to give away was kind of a weird moment. But I was just happy it went to a good home. When a childless friend who was shopping for a baby shower gift asked me, "What would you most want with you on a desert island, if you had the kids along?, I immediately thought of the jog stroller. We'd do laps around the island and be grateful and happy to have the exercise.

Boston Globe – January 24, 2008

A mother finds it's possible to combine her best selves

by Nancy Shohet West

I expected to be the type of mother who would get sentimental about giving up baby items. I thought I'd find the dispersal of tiny clothes and infant toys to be poignant.

But as the younger of my two children outgrew the paraphernalia of infancy, I found simple relief and a sense of catharsis in shucking off the old and looking ahead to the new. Boxing up my maternity clothes meant no more morning sickness. Leaving the changing table at the swap shed reminded me that I was done with dirty diapers.

It wasn't until I thought about giving up my jog stroller that sentimentality struck.

Unlike nursing pads and teething rings, the jog stroller embodied all my favorite parts of raising young children. Long a recreational runner, I gave up running for the first time in my adult life when my first child was born. Due to a combination of doctor's orders and the obvious limitations that caring for a newborn put on my time and energy, running became something from my past.

And I never acknowledged how much I missed it until the Mother's Day eight months after my son Tim's birth, when my husband surprised me with a gift-wrapped box the size of our coffee table. A photo on the front of the box showed a cheerful, fit young woman dressed in workout wear and pushing her beaming tot down a sunlit street.

"I can go running – *and* care for the baby?" I marveled. It was as unimaginable a feat to me as living in two different time periods at once.

The jog stroller became the most indispensable tool in my parenting tool kit. My son loved being taken out for a run. Back then we lived in a suburban neighborhood with wide sidewalks and plenty of people out working in their yards on nice days, many of whom remembered seeing me run before the baby's arrival.

"You're back," they would say amicably. "I'm back," I'd reply with overwhelming relief.

There were so many ways in which I'd become unrecognizable to myself since the baby was born: the way I dressed, the books I read, the pediatrician appointments and playgroups with which I filled my day. But when I was out running, I briefly became the person I was before.

By the time Tim started kindergarten, our second child had just grown big enough to sit upright. With the jog stroller, I could walk Tim to school every day, rolling the baby along with us. (And, in the interest of full disclosure, I admit that I let Tim perch on the stroller's foot rest on the many days that he protested about the mile-long walk.)

Nonetheless, I'm not sorry my kids are now too big for the stroller. Tim, whom I first brought along on a 3-mile run when he was 8 months old, can now run a 3-miler alongside me.

Holly, as an independent and determined kindergartner, would rather push a stroller than ride in one. But I held on to it because I wanted it to go to someone who would love it as much as I did.

And then my friend Marilyn mentioned that she had a new grandchild. Marilyn's son – father of the new baby – is a marathon runner, and I imagined with delight my stroller out training for the Boston Marathon.

But Marilyn had a better idea than passing it on to her son. Why not take the stroller for her own use? Her grandchild lives out of state, but whenever he visits, Marilyn can take him on long trail walks or neighborhood strolls in my old jogger.

It was a win-win solution. My stroller went to a good home, just as I'd hoped.

Still, I was a little sad to see it go. It had once served as a bridge between my pre-baby and post-baby self. As any mother knows, that's a pretty hefty task for something as unassuming as a metal frame and nylon seat on three tires.

I was a runner long before I was a parent, and for a few postpartum months the two personae seemed irreconcilable. Seeing the stroller now reminds me of the elation I felt when I first saw a glimmer of possibility that the two women might in fact be the same person.

Tim's running log: 1/30, 7:30 PM. Day 172. 1.4 miles. Moon so bright on the snow we could see our shadows!

When we started running, I wanted the running to solve all of our problems, all of our weird problematic mother-son interdynamics and all of Tim's moodiness issues. And then I'd be periodically disappointed when that didn't happen: he was still sullen or, as still happened regularly, he went out of his way to irritate me.

But this is what I was beginning to acknowledge: while it's true that running isn't magic, as I'd reminded myself again and again, what it *had* done was given us something in common and a daily touchstone of what we liked to do together. No matter how moody Tim was being or how cross I became, we knew we were going to go running together and we knew we were probably going to get along well during the run.

So there precisely was the value of streak running together: not that it was a magic bullet, but that it gave us a daily dose of fairy dust, a daily interlude in which we were together and happy. Even if it was just fifteen minutes long. And the fact was that even if Tim and I got along beautifully only fifteen minutes a day, it was still every single day.

And it reminded me of that most fundamental truth about parents and children: no matter how they treat us, we love them. No matter how hard it gets, we love our children. Analogously, no matter how badly we were getting along, we were gonna do that run together. Every day.

GUEST RUNNERS AND THEIR HOMETOWNS 1/31/08
Nathan B. - Carlisle, MA
John M. - Washington, DC
John L. - Nashua, NH
Eric M. - Carlisle, MA
Nicole P. - Carlisle, MA
Austin P. - Carlisle, MA
Sophie R. - Swarthmore, PA
Alyssa A. - Sandwich, MA

DOGS
Angus P. - Carlisle, MA

STUFFED ANIMALS
Ba, a frog – Carlisle, MA

Every now and then I would look at Tim and feel a little bit incredulous about his aerobic capabilities. A year earlier he'd never run a nonstop mile, and now he was really such a good runner. It wasn't about speed or distance; it was just that he was developing terrific endurance. It was probably something most kids his age could do if they tried; I just didn't see that many trying.

It made me think about how kids really amaze us with what they're capable of from the time they're born. The fact that they can latch on to a breast seems amazing; the fact that they can nurse until they have enough sustenance to survive and grow is hard to believe at first. Tim used to amaze me by lying in his crib gazing at a mobile until he fell asleep at night when he was an infant. Holly amazed me as a kindergartener by being able to sound out words. And Tim was amazing me anew by being able to run five miles without a peep of complaint.

That was one of the best things about being a parent, I decided: all those times when our kids surprised us with their capabilities. It was a wondrous thing.

Early in February there was a seven-alarm fire in Lawrence – an economically depressed city about twenty miles north of us – that caused one hundred and fifty people to have to

119

evacuate. I kept thinking of those poor people, forced out onto the street in the middle of a ten-degree night. It was so fortunate no one was hurt – including no firefighters – but how awful. Imagine being out in the cold, your children crying and uncomfortable, watching your home burn, no idea of where to go, no idea of what you'd lost, no idea of what to do next, and cold, cold, cold.

I had been thinking a lot about what it would be like to be homeless in this weather. Because it could so easily happen. In a way, knowing what I know now, I wonder how anyone can choose to have children, not because they're a lot of work but because you incur so much risk when you have people to take care of. We had a good support system, but it seemed to me that even *we* could end up homeless. Suppose my parents were no longer living, and we couldn't make our mortgage payments, and the bank foreclosed on our house. Well, of course, it was easy to say "If things got bad enough we'd sell our house, and then we'd have plenty of money," but what if we couldn't sell the house?

Or what would it be like to have to keep your whole family in your car? Because even with a car, how would you heat it in this weather? One night back when we still lived in Framingham, I stopped off on my way home late one evening to pick up some milk at our neighborhood convenience store. The only other car in the small parking lot had its engine running and seemed to be full of children. When I walked inside, the store looked empty, and then a clerk came in from the parking lot, and I realized she must have been in that car. After I paid and left, she followed me back out.

As I mulled over this strange scenario afterwards, it seemed possible that her family was in the car not because they were homeless but because she didn't have childcare that night, but who knows? Maybe they were all planning to spend the night in the car because they had nowhere else to sleep.

A reporter I know wrote a story about a woman who went homeless on Christmas Eve. Imagine, even if you've managed to buy just a few gifts for your kids, taking them out on the street and it's Christmas Eve and you're thinking that you have to drag along your few presents to give them the next day, but you still won't have any place to live. It's such a scary, scary thing.

Tim's journal
Feb. 6, 2008
Today my mom and I are at 179 days of running! I don't like running on ice, but I like running in snow. We've run one race but we're gonna run more races in the spring. When it was icy we kept having to run up and down the driveway. Now since the ice and most of the snow have melted we run on the footpaths (which makes us be able to do a lot more different runs). The hardest day for me so far was in January. It was seven degrees, but with the wind chill it was minus 5 with the wind blowing right in our faces which made it feel minus 20 degrees. My mom's goal is to get to one year but my goal is to get to 70 years.

I kept hearing Tim tell people his streak-running goal was seventy years. I wished I knew whether he really meant that or whether he was just saying it for effect. Did he really think he'd want to run every day for seventy years? Every day of school, college, adult life, until he was seventy-nine years old? I couldn't imagine feeling that way. But maybe he did, or maybe he had no idea of what a range of years seven decades would actually cover.

He was correct in what he wrote in his school journal, *my* goal was one year. One year of daily miles. But we weren't even halfway through the year yet. All that running, all the ice and snow and wind we'd gone through, and we were not even halfway – that was hard for me to grasp.

In the middle of February, despite my attempts to put my best foot forward at work and show some tangible improvement, a mistake arose so grave that I nearly had an anxiety attack in the office bathroom. In short, a vendor was charging us for $50,000 in unpaid fees, and no one could figure out how the previous invoices had gone unpaid. My manager was sure they had been sent to me, though I couldn't imagine how I could have overlooked them.

The vendor was the company that translates our materials for our European offices. Joan didn't have her own administrative assistant, but she also did not usually expect me to do clerical work. Normally when invoices arrived, she would open them with her other mail, fill out the necessary paperwork that our accounting office required in order to pay them, and then hand them on to me to make copies and file, since the filing cabinet happened to be located in my workspace. So it puzzled me that she was blaming me for this oversight, and raised the question in my mind as to whether she was looking for something convenient to pin on me.

It forced me to spend quite a lot of time thinking about what I'd do if I lost my job. If I lost my job, we definitely wouldn't be able to make our mortgage payments, and we couldn't sell our house in the current market, so we'd go into foreclosure. That thought terrified me. I could look for another job, but I imagined I'd be very unlikely to come close to my current salary and I didn't know how easy it would be to find a position at all, nor did I know how the mistake in question would impede me from finding another job.

I tried to convince myself that surely it wouldn't make sense for me to get fired. No one was accusing me of *stealing* the $50,000; we just couldn't figure out where the invoices had gone and why they hadn't been submitted.

But if the company fired me, I reasoned, they'd have to find someone else to do my job, and that would cost them time and money as well and just couldn't be the best solution. At the same time, I knew that in business, when screw-ups happen, heads roll. Even I understood that.

Tim's running log: 2/12, 7:15 PM. Day 185. 1.4 miles. Couple inches of light fluffy powdery snow on top of icy crust. The crust was so thick we could both run on top of it, which was fun.

Tim had an assignment to write in his school journal about how he imagined the perfect vacation. And guess what his perfect vacation was? A trip to a beachside mansion in Florida with Rick. *Alone* with Rick. According to the description he drafted, it had an indoor football arena, indoor basketball court, baseball field, game room, TV room, seafood restaurant next door for dinner and private chef for lunch – but no Mom in sight. I had to admit that it hurt my feelings slightly. Why not all of that bling *and* Mom?

It brought me right back to where I was when we started running together: convinced I had to find a way to avoid that same expression my friend had used about her family member: Those two are like oil and water. *Not my son and me,* I had insisted to myself. So we'd started going running together. Every day. And it had been great. But then I find out his ideal vacation leaves me two thousand miles behind. Thanks, pal.

CHAPTER 7

February 13 – March 12, 2008

Ever since I met Rick, I've mentally divided the couples I know into two categories: those who met by organized circumstance and those who met by random coincidence. Rick and I are in the latter camp. I attended a women's college in Boston that still, in the late 1980s, held old-fashioned mixers to which the boys from the college down the street were invited. At one such mixer, I happened to be crossing in front of Rick as his roommate turned from the dance floor to motion to him, and I was in the way, and that alone caused us to strike up a conversation. It was a big crowded room; if I had paused for thirty seconds before walking past, or if he had dropped his drink at the moment his roommate turned toward him, or if either of us had gone to a different party that night, we never would have met.

In the other camp – organized circumstance – are people who, if they hadn't met on Monday, would have met on Tuesday. My older sister met her husband when they lived in the same freshman dorm. My parents met because my father's best friend was dating my mother's roommate. My in-laws met because my father-in-law's brother was dating my mother-in-law's best friend. A very large number of my friends met their spouses either in college or in the workplace, and several of the couples I admire most for the apparent strength of their relationship have known each other since high school or even earlier.

In other words, there wasn't a stroke of random fate or a moment of split-second timing involved – they had dozens if not hundreds of chances to run in to each other, or there were people determined to introduce them. If my father had decided not to stop by my mother's apartment with his buddy on April 19th, 1961, their friends still would have seen to it that they met some other day that month, or that year, or whenever.

I used to find it thrilling that Rick and I met so randomly. But sometimes now I find it alarming that I know so few other examples of married couples who met by coincidence. Sometimes I worry there's a message in it: you aren't *supposed* to meet someone if your paths cross for only a second or two. You're supposed to meet someone whom fate has put you in continuous proximity with, at a job or in a dorm or in an apartment building or in a social club or wherever. Surely this coincidence can't bode well for us.

But we're happy together. It's just puzzling to me, and I guess a sign of aging, that what once seemed marvelously romantic now seems a little, well, dubious. Maybe as you get older, it's normal to try to see the universe as a more organized structure, whereas when you're in your twenties it's fun to think that everything exciting happens randomly. Maybe as you get older, you start to see how potentially problematic that could be. But for us it seems to work. It just doesn't seem like quite the magical tale that it once did…more like a stroke of good luck, at best, than a stroke of Cinderella's fairy godmother's magic wand.

Tim's running log: 2/13, 6:30 PM. Day 186. 1.1 miles. Six months!!!!!

At work, I had my yearly review, and it turned out I was in an even worse position than I'd imagined. By the time it ended, I felt as if I'd sat through an hour-long discussion for which the tagline could have been "Are you stupid, or are you lazy?"

I knew my manager was right that I hadn't been proactive enough in going after stories, and in saying that I do more copy

126

editing and revising than crafting and writing. But there was no acknowledgment of how frosty our relations had been. There was no explanation for why she just didn't seem to *like* me anymore. And it just left me feeling awful.

It was like a breakup or a divorce, I would imagine – even if you're resigned to what has happened and what the likely outcome is, it's still sad to view the damage that time hath wrought. Joan and I were so happy together in the beginning. She was pleased with my work and we got along well. Even if I could resuscitate the quality of my work, I didn't think I could get the relationship we had, or that I had with the company, back.

Tim's running log: 2/14, 7 PM. Day 187. 1.2 miles. Ice was horrible. My mom could hardly run at all and even I had trouble. BUT we didn't fall!

As the ice problem grew worse, there were nights when I felt like I was barely moving, just mincing along in the slowest jog possible that still carried enough motion and momentum to count as a jog rather than a walk.

Meanwhile, Tim still loped along. Sometimes he even ran forward and doubled back just to keep me company as I inched by. I kept trying to tell myself to just run in Tim's tracks and I'd be fine, but instead I'd find myself almost immobilized with fear of falling. For the first time all year, I began to think that it might simply not be possible to run every day of the year; there might be days we just physically couldn't.

Despite these thoughts, we persisted. Some nights, my glacial jog averaged out at a fifteen-minute mile. But we did it anyway.

Leaving full-time salaried work altogether, though long a dream of mine, seemed completely out of the picture for the future. Despite my fantasies earlier in the year that maybe we'd be able to live off my freelance and Rick's consulting income in the near future, that no longer felt to me like what was going to happen. Instead, I began to acknowledge that if I was lucky, I could stay at the biosciences company indefinitely, until a better job came along. If I was *unlucky*, I'd lose my job, and then we'd have a disaster on our hands.

But the ice problem on our running route did give me a handy metaphor to live by that winter. With my job, just as with the ice, I kept reminding myself: *Spring lies ahead. Look to the thaw, look to the thaw. The ice will yield to mud; then the sun will come out, and soon we'll be running on beautiful dry summer roadways. And maybe the ice will thaw and the mud will clear at work also.*

As winter wore on, Rick began talking with increasing insistence about beginning the process for weight loss surgery.

When he first brought up the idea of weight loss surgery, right after Christmas, I didn't think he was serious. Plastic surgery is not popular in our circles; our friends wear blue jeans and fleece, and their idea of personal pampering is a massage after a triathlon, not liposuction or tummy tucks.

Moreover, weight control had always been a bit of a sore subject between us, He's not a big overeater, but he's not an exerciser either. "Just do what I do!" I've wanted to tell him so many times throughout the past twenty years. "Don't eat fast food. Exercise every day. Look at me! That's all it takes!"

But for him, it's never worked. Even when he starts exercise regimes or diets, it doesn't make much difference. He is just a naturally heavy person, and he comes from a genetically overweight family, which doesn't help.

I never really thought about weight loss surgery as an answer. That was partly because until Rick started researching it, I didn't know our insurance would pay for it. But it was also a sense that it was such an extreme response to what I believed was a fairly easy problem to control. *Just do what I do*: Isn't that on some level the subtext of every marital dispute? *Why can't you be more like me* – isn't that the question we are always silently asking our spouses, whether the topic is fiscal management, child rearing or religious practices?

Just be like me, I wanted to say to Rick. *It's not about genetics or luck; it's about being willing to get on the stationary bike for 45 minutes every morning.*

But as Rick continued pursuing his research, I could see he actually believed there might be an alternative to obesity in his future. And he was feeling more optimistic about his consulting business, as well. Sensing such happy vibes from him made me feel better. We had gone through some difficult times together and it was looking like dawn might be breaking.

Tim's running log: 2/17: 3 PM. Day 190. 2.2 miles. We went up to Church Street so that we could run on dry pavement. Mom couldn't keep up with me.

After a particularly enjoyable evening of frosting cupcakes, putting away laundry and being with the kids, I went outside to gaze at the night sky and had a flash of insight. That phrase, "our days are numbered," popped into my head, and I began thinking about how that idea is really what's behind so much of my sentiment about work. Our days are numbered; I therefore just couldn't get too worked up about whether I'm showing the proper level of professional commitment by touring our Portsmouth site or drafting a profile of the CEO. Every day, we all have one fewer day on earth than we had the day before, and that's something you really need to spend carefully.

I needed my job because I wanted to be able to support my family, live in our house, and so on. So it wasn't like I could give it up altogether. But I knew I needed to keep a healthy sense of perspective too. My days are numbered, just like everyone's are, and although the invoice problem was in the end a positive eye-opener about wanting to keep my job, in general I can't let every day be a big overwhelming drama.

Tim's running log: 2/27, 6:10 AM. Day 200. 2 miles. We are at 200 days!!! We've started running in the morning again. This morning there was cold slush on the ground and our feet got soaked, but the sky was pretty, turning pink as the sun rose.

Tim admitted that he couldn't believe we still had a half-year to go before reaching our one-year goal. I had been feeling the same way. As proud as we both were to reach the six-month mark, in some ways it was overwhelming to think that meant we still had an equal amount of time to cover as what we'd already done.

I reminded him that we'd surely been through the toughest weather of the year. Early spring might be muddy and rainy; late spring would be buggy; early summer would be humid; and midsummer would be hot; but we'd run through ice and snow, and surely no other weather conditions would be more challenging than what we'd done.

Then, since he had been so honest with me, I admitted that if I had known what this winter would be like in terms of weather, I'd never have suggested we try to run a streak. There had been snow on the ground and freezing temperatures since December 1, with only two notable thaws. This winter wouldn't set records for snowfall, but it certainly had been consistent: relentlessly cold, snowy and icy.

But as I kept saying, no one would be impressed if we streak-ran through a mild winter, would they?

Tim's running log: 3/13, 6:45 PM. Day 215. 1.5 miles. Ran to Bedford Rd. crosswalk and back. Ice is gone so we can run on the footpath! So it's getting fun again!!

CHAPTER 8

March 14 – April 14, 2008

Analogies between parenting and running repeatedly struck me. One evening as I was wearing the headlamp, which casts a small, somewhat dim spotlight that reflects puddles and ice patches but doesn't illuminate the surroundings well at all, Tim was running just ahead of me, so I was trying to keep the light aimed about ten feet in front of him. Sometimes I could get it just where I wanted it. Other times I found myself shining it right on the back of his jacket, which was no use to him at all and not very helpful to me. And once in a while I would forget to aim it at all and ended up shining it into the trees or at some random point off the side of the road.

As a parent, mostly you try to shed light for your kid on what's just ahead in the road, knowing you can't illuminate every possible stone that he could trip over but trying to at least reflect the big puddles and the obvious branches in the path – casting light on those significant obstacles as he makes his way along. But sometimes you get so fixated on your child himself that you shine the light right on his back and just stare at him and don't illuminate a thing for anyone. And still other times you lose focus altogether and shine your light on some random place in the future – with thoughts like "Maybe if we go to church every week, you'll grow up with some kind of moral compass" – but it seems pretty random and not a whole lot of immediate help when he ends up stumbling over a frozen rut in the middle of the path anyway.

Tim's running log: 3/15, 1:30 PM. Day 217. 4.1 miles. My mom wanted to go on a long run so we went down to Owen and Hugh's house and around there. I was kind of bored.

By mid-March, the long winter seemed finally to be subsiding. Tim commented one evening on our run, "I really think winter is over. Well, I shouldn't say that, because I don't want to curse it…" and I thought that was so funny, that he had that sort of old-lady-ish notion that you curse your luck by assuming the best. I just didn't think kids thought that way.

Meanwhile, I was putting all my mental energy into keeping my job. I couldn't imagine that a huge turnaround was going to happen that would make me love the bioscience field, but I wanted to be in a position again where I could feel good about my work. Part of me could imagine getting a much better review next year, one in which it was agreed that I really came through on my part of the deal, made great efforts, changed one hundred eighty degrees. But another part of me said, *Look, my goal right now is to stay employed, that's all. I just cannot afford to get fired.*

Tim's running log: 3/16, 5 PM. Day 218. 1.8 miles. I only wanted to do a short run, but it was fun and easy. AND we saw Holly's kindergarten teacher!

Early spring always feels like a great part of the school calendar to me. The newness of school that you deal with in the fall is no longer an issue, and the fever pitch of holiday preparations is far behind as well. This is the part of the year when all the focus seems to be on accomplishing what needs to be accomplished. And I was feeling a little bit nostalgic about the fact that this was the last time I'd have a kindergartener immersed in kindergarten spring. I look at my niece, Sophie, and the teens who are my friends' children, and wonder how their mothers can bear to have them so close to moving into adulthood, and college. Meanwhile I look at pregnant colleagues and other women whose stints as parents are only just beginning and feel so thankful that I don't still have all that ahead, all the worry and uncertainty and boredom of caring for babies and toddlers. Surely this must be the best phase of all, the elementary school parenting years.

Tim's running log: 3/20, 7 PM. Day 222. 1.2 miles. First day of spring!!! Full moon. The moonlight shining on the clouds looked very unusual.

Joan traveled a lot in March. The peace and quiet that her absence afforded me was little comfort when the tradeoff was an in-box full of negativity every morning. I'd boot up and sit down with a weary sigh, clicking through them one by one. "What could you have possibly been thinking as far as story order on this week's newsletter?" "How could you have suggested that we run the Q&A for the press conference separate from the story?" "Did you even *try* to find a better subject for this week's employee profile than the one you used?"

I was convinced that I should stitch myself a sampler that said "Are you lazy, or are you stupid?" And yet I knew her fundamental complaint about me was accurate: without a stronger interest in the life sciences, I just couldn't get good at my job.

Tim's running log: 3/24, 5:45 PM. Day 226. 1.5 miles. We ran before dinner because it was still light out! It looks like spring!!

With the milder temperatures and longer hours of daylight, Tim's disposition improved dramatically: the flip side of the Seasonal Affective Disorder, I guess. As we went running before dinner one evening well before sunset, he chattered away. He told me about lunch with his teacher from last year – a monthly event at which each kid reports on what's new in his or her life – and Tim remembered every item: Paige's guinea pig died. Elena is going on a weekend trip with her parents. Emma is getting a dog, David's basement flooded. He told me about the game of wall-ball they played at recess ("I know this doesn't really interest you, Mom, but I made forty-two catches"). He told me about what they learned in music class (how to play the scale tone "la" on the recorder), and six or seven other important items.

And even though I was only half listening, what I kept thinking was *This. Is. Why. We. Run.* Tim was in such a good mood, so happy to be outdoors, and so chatty. It was all that I hoped for when we embarked on this admittedly absurd challenge. I felt like saying, "Stop and look at what we're doing. Never mind all those awful icy nights in December or the heavy rains last week...or any of the times it was just so hard to get out of the door. This evening: sunlight, springtime ahead, reviewing the day of a third grader. This is the point."

Wiffle ball was in some ways what put an end to my days as a stay-at-home mom. Well, no, the need to pay our bills was what put an end to that. But when I think back to the days that I was home full-time with the kids, I remember the best of it – sunny autumn afternoons at the playground just gabbing with my friends while all the kids had fun together – and the worst of it – Tim eternally pleading with me to play a few more minutes of wiffle ball.

That's part of what I found hard about dealing with Tim at times: his tendency to ask, ask, ask. An image that seems to be lodged in my head is from a summer day when he was seven or eight and we had been at the beach since late morning, visiting my college roommate and her family at their vacation house in southern Maine. We go once or twice every summer to visit them. It's less than two hours from Carlisle, and since she has a full house already with four kids, we usually opt for a day trip rather than an overnight.

We had spent the whole day playing there. We'd had a cookout on the lawn and played beach badminton and splashed in the tidal pools and waded in the surf and dug in the sand. On the way home, we stopped for a fried clam dinner.

Sated with sun and sand and exercise and seafood, all of us except for Rick, who was driving, fell sound asleep on the way home. And then as we pulled into the garage, Tim woke up, looked around, and said "Mom, will you play wiffle ball with me now?"

Wiffle ball? I wanted to say. *Now? After everything we've done today, after all the fun we've had, you're still asking for wiffle ball?*

I know it's just what kids do, and of course if he was asking for something that came a little more naturally to me – like reading a story, say – I wouldn't have taken it so hard. But it's wiffle ball that seems to represent everything demanding about Tim. Ask, ask, ask. Never feel satisfied. After a day at the beach, still be wanting to play wiffle ball. I felt like I was forever saying *No, not now, too much to do, maybe later, just don't feel like it.*

Tim's running log: 3/25, 7 PM. Day 227. 1.1 miles. A little windy but still nice to be running in daylight.

As we were running down our driveway one evening, I pulled a tissue out of my pocket...and a second one tumbled out and blew off to the side of the road. Not wanting to double back, I said I'd pick it up on the return trip.

"Mom, you're littering!" Tim exclaimed with a tone of somewhat thrilled horror. "That was a *textbook* case of littering!"

Where he came up with the expression "textbook case" was not clear to me. "I'll pick it up on the way home!" I said defensively.

"It will have blown away by then! Mom, every piece of litter causes a half-inch of ice to melt!" he informed me. "I learned that on the Discovery Channel."

135

Huh. So there I was, trying to do a good thing by taking my son for a daily run, and instead I was contributing to global warming and the ruin of the polar ice cap.

On the way home we *did* spot my Kleenex, and I picked it up. So no penguins would die in my name on that day.

On a brighter note, we then heard geese honking overhead. "That's my favorite sound at this time of year," Tim said. "It means spring is coming."

Funny, because we don't really like geese that much once they arrive . . . they make such a mess on the lawn. But any sign of spring was welcome at that point.

Tim's running log: 3/26, 8:30 PM. Day 228. 1.2 miles. Not feeling too good, but I was okay to run.

Tim was a little under the weather for a few days, but insisted that he still wanted to run. He knew that Ron Kmiec, our streak-running role model, once ran with several broken ribs, so he said not feeling great wasn't going to slow *us* down. (The way he actually put it was "Mom, we ain't no BABIES!")

I knew it was questionable judgment, but so was the streak. At that point, my attitude was "In for a penny, in for a pound." Having encouraged my child to run for the past two hundred twenty-eight consecutive days, I couldn't suddenly pretend to be a paragon of excellent judgment. And if we *did* make it a year, no one was going to believe that in a full year, neither of us ever felt unwell. So yes, I let him run when he was feeling under the weather. He had eaten a big dinner, and loss of appetite is usually a good indicator of how sick a kid is, so I really didn't think anything much was wrong.

Halfway through our 1.2-mile course, he said in sort of a croaky way, "Mommm..." and I thought he was about to admit he wasn't feeling well enough to continue, but instead he started telling me about a debate his class had concerning paper bags versus plastic bags and how his classmate Claire had informed them that it takes one thousand years for a plastic bag to disintegrate. Every day is Earth Day when you're in the third grade.

With snow and cold weather revisiting us several times during March, I thought often of a line by Amby Burfoot, legendary marathon runner and executive editor of *Runner's World*. In one of his books he says something like "There is NO kind of weather that is not enjoyable for running. Well, okay, if there's ONE kind of weather that's not enjoyable to run in, it would be thirty-four degrees and raining, but everything else is fine for running!"

I felt like Tim and I had run in thirty-four degrees and raining at least once a week all winter. We were tired of it. I kept trying to picture the warm, sunny spring day on which I hoped we'd run the 5-mile Pennsylvania race in mid-April.

Even with the days growing longer, and all the fresh air we were getting, Tim still went through waves of pallid catatonia. One Saturday he and Rick spent the morning outside burning brush and I thought he was having a good time, but afterwards he looked even more pallid and spoke more quietly than usual. It just seemed to me that nothing could clear up that tendency of his toward melancholy. We'd go out for a run, and for twenty minutes he'd be cheerful and energetic, but when we returned, he'd melt into the corner of the couch again.

As much as I tried to make things change for him, and the running was really just one big attempt to do that, at times it didn't seem like things had improved at all. It was back to kindergarten, when if he wasn't allowed video games and I wasn't available for wiffle ball, he'd just plain melt into the couch.

With parent-teacher conferences scheduled for late March, I thought about asking Tim's teacher about it, but I'd tried that with other teachers in past years and had yet to find a teacher who perceived the concerns about Tim that I did. Still, I figured they at least must know what childhood depression or bipolar disorder looks like. Surely we could at least start with that.

I feared that if I asked a mental health specialist, they would by definition see something wrong, something that required treatment of some kind; I believed that a teacher would be more objective. What I really wanted, in this case, was for Tim to be compared with other kids his age; I wanted to know if he seemed markedly more melancholy than other nine-year-old boys in Carlisle. To anyone other than me.

Tim's running log: 3/31, 10 AM. Day 233. 3.3 miles. Mom wanted to do more; I wanted to do less.

As I was reading *Winnie the Pooh* to Holly before bed one night, she plunked down into my lap, and I put my arms around her, and we just started hugging and rocking, and she kept saying "More hugging! More hugging!" And it seemed so important to me not to let the moment end, to just sit there with her. We were both so comfortable and so happy.

Any time the kids inexplicably cleave onto me like that, I find myself wondering if maybe they know something I don't, if they are being guided by a kind of prescience, knowing we soon won't be able to hold each other like that again. I think about how if I perished tomorrow, or even if I live another fifty years, either way, Holly might remember how it felt to be held and hugged and rocked that night; that might be how she always remembers me. Or even if that wasn't her *entire* memory of me –she might just as easily remember how cross I always am on Sunday mornings when we're getting ready for church – she'd still have that memory to balance it.

I found myself thinking of two really morbid stories that had been in the news in the past couple of years. A journalist on

138

Cape Cod had been murdered in her home, and she was found with her daughter cuddled against the body. And then there was an even stranger story a few years ago about a little girl whose mother died of natural causes one evening while sitting in an easy chair, but the two of them were the only ones in the house and the girl still did what she always did in the evening, spent the night in her mother's arms with the TV on.

Both girls just wanted, and achieved, one last stint of snuggling against their moms, and that's how they were found by adults later on. Both of them knew something was wrong – the journalist's daughter was too little to understand what; she must have just been horrified to realize her mother would not wake; but the other child had gone to school and said to a classmate that her mother seemed to be dead, and she clearly knew she should have gone for help – but both of them still wanted the comfort one last time of their mothers' skin against theirs.

So on the occasions that Holly just wants to be hugged and rocked, that's what I do.

Tim's running log: 4/2, 6:30 PM. Day 235. 1.2 miles. I wish all the puddles would dry up.

One of my editors at the *Globe* suggested I do a follow-up story on Ronald Kmiec, describing his rehabilitation after the heart attack and his determination to return to the Boston Marathon for the thirty-fourth consecutive year. He had resumed running in late December after taking six weeks off.

I interviewed him at his home on a Saturday afternoon. After I was done asking him questions, he and I started discussing Tim. "It will teach him great self-discipline," Ronald said. "It will give him skills that will help him in other areas as well." Then he asked, "What is it doing for *you*?"

Funny how strange it felt to have anyone asking about *me*. It wasn't just the usual thing that moms are always focused on other people rather than vice versa. It was also that as a writer, I'm always out interviewing people about their lives, roles, perspectives, concerns ... and so seldom on the other end of that equation.

So when he asked, I had to stop and think about it. What *had* our running streak done for me? Given me at least fifteen minutes a day alone with Tim when we were doing something we both enjoyed and not arguing about anything. Put me in closer contact with the outdoors: not only the weather conditions, of which we were constantly aware, but also the sunrise/sunset schedule, phases of the moon, groundwater levels. Helped me to see a side of Tim that was more committed, focused and ambitious than what I usually saw in him. Made me commit to doing something with no tangible gain, day after day, when I felt like it and when I didn't. Helped me improve at striking a compromise with Tim, when he wanted to do one distance or route and I wanted to do another.

What it had *not* done for me: caused any weight loss!

Tim's running log: 4/6, 2:30 PM. Day 239. 4.2 miles. We did a long run because it was a nice day. We did the "Owen and Hugh Loop" which is called that because we pass my friends Owen and Hugh's house.

While Tim and I were running together on the gravel path around the Cranberry Bog, he jostled against me and then I slightly bumped him back but hit my elbow. Tim said, "This is *exactly* like something that happened in a Celtics game I watched earlier this week! Ray Allen handed the ball off to Kendrick Perkins, and Kendrick Perkins turned quickly to pass it back to him, and Ray Allen bumped against him and hit his funny bone really hard."

I commented to him that this was the first and almost definitely the last time that *anything* I had done had been compared to midcourt action during a Celtics game.

Finally, in the second week of April, we had a spring thaw, not just seasonably mild but *un*-seasonably mild, with temperatures up to seventy degrees in the middle of the afternoon for a couple of days. After months of layering on the fleece and hats and face masks and gloves, it was wonderful to run in tights and a sweatshirt.

And it was tempting to be overly metaphorical, to say *Oh look, we made it through all the ice and snow and frigid temperatures and wind chill and now we're running in sweet mild springtime air with the sound of peepers behind us. The cold winter weather is over, we ran right through it, and we made it into beautiful sunny springtime.* It would be so easy to believe we'd weathered the worst of the storms and now it was all going to be easy.

But of course, there was one catch: seasons are cyclical, not linear, and so is just about everything for which I might try to build an analogy to the seasons. Whether the topic was my ability to relate to Tim, his propensity toward crankiness, Holly's occasional lapses into toddler-like behavior, family tensions, health concerns (of which we blessedly had none at the moment, but it's not something you ever really feel far from), it was all cyclical. You could never just say "We made it through the awful winter weather and now it's spring," you could only say "What a beautiful spring day *this* was and how lucky we were to have it, no matter whether the next spate of bad weather arrives next week or not until next winter."

CHAPTER 9

April 12 – May 11, 2008

Reaching our eight-month anniversary of streak running meant more to me than reaching our six-month anniversary had. At six months, Tim and I made a big deal about how we'd been running for half a year. But when that date actually came, in mid-February, I think we both felt more a sense of incredulity than triumph: sure, we'd accomplished a half-year of daily running, but as challenging as it had been, we still had to do the whole thing over again in order to reach our goal of one year.

Eight months, on the other hand, felt like getting over the hump. At that point, even my non-mathematical brain could conceptualize the fractions behind it: we had run *two* days for every *one* day left to go. (I continued to hold one year up as my goal, whereas Tim still said his was seventy years.) Moreover, the four months that remained would take us from mid-April to mid-August, which compared to the winter we'd been through sounded so promising from a meteorological perspective.

Nonetheless, a part of me still felt like in terms of the goal of not missing a day of running, our odds were no better at eight months than they had been at six months or even four, though I understood that mathematically that wasn't true. On any given day, I felt like there was still the same number of things that could disrupt our plans, except that weather was less of a factor in spring than in winter.

One morning before school, for example, Holly was bitten by a tick. Lyme disease is a prevalent problem in our area, perhaps because of all the deer that inhabit the thickly forested areas of Carlisle. She showed no problematic symptoms, but it reminded me that if Tim got Lyme disease, that would certainly put an end to our running. And so could a lot of other physical problems, no matter how committed to the goal we might both claim to be.

Tim's running log: 4/13, 4 PM. Day 246. 2.8 miles. Kind of chilly but pretty nice compared to winter.

I worried that Tim hadn't taken the training for our upcoming five-mile race seriously enough. He hadn't run five miles since late fall; he hadn't even done very many four-mile runs since the snow first fell in early December.

But my friend Nancy tried to give me some perspective on it when I complained to her that I didn't really think Tim was ready for the race. "Your way of training for a five-mile race would be to do a bunch of five-mile runs leading up to it," she said. "Tim's way of training for a five-mile race is to do some shorter runs and then do the race on adrenaline and finish it just fine."

And I knew she was right. Tim and I had the same goal – to have a good run and enjoy the race and not find it too taxing or exhausting – but our ways of approaching it were different. I'd train for it by *simulating* it, running several other five-mile courses; Tim was training for it simply by resolving in his own mind that he was going to *do* it.

It came down once again to that three-word motto by which almost all of my great parenting revelations could be reduced. *He's. Not. You.* Our kids are not our clones. Even when we amaze ourselves by getting them interested in the same things we're interested in, as had happened with Tim and me in terms of running, they're not going to approach it the same way.

Tim's running log: 4/15. 6:45 PM. Day 248. 1.2 miles. Ran through the cemetery again.

The more Tim and I worked on distances, the more I began to think that I wasn't in the prime condition I wanted to believe I was in. My muscles weren't as strong as I wished; my stamina wasn't as high. I could do the mileage, but that was about all; in general, I suspected my body wasn't really up for what I was trying to do.

And there was no excuse for that. Nicole had been working with a trainer for the past year and looked fabulous, toned and strong and lean as well as naturally beautiful. I certainly couldn't afford a trainer, but it did make me realize that I was negligent when it came to everything except aerobic exercise. Surely some leg work would improve my running.

Tim's running log: 4/16, 7:15 PM. Day 249. 1.5 miles. Just ran on the common driveway because we were already tired and it was getting late.

My friend Amy, whom I've known since high school, called me to say her mother had died after a one-and-a-half-year struggle with pancreatic cancer. Amy's mother wasn't young, but it reinforced my sense that illness and demise were all around me, and I kept trying to decide whether that's a natural part of growing older – entering my forties, it seemed logical I'd be nearer to more cases of illness than I was in my thirties – or whether, indeed, there were a coincidentally large number of cases of illness in the circles around me.

Right after Amy's mother died, another high school friend of ours, Courtney, lost her father. When I talked with Courtney at the wake, she started to cry as she said that her last visit with her dad was so hard because he was so unhappy: uncomfortable and contentious. When someone who is well into their seventies, like both of my friends' parents, dies of illness, it's easy to talk about a life well-lived and dying in peace, but when you realize that in fact those last days can be excruciating for the person and those surrounding him or her alike, I find it so hard to feel okay about the process.

Not that it would be better if everyone died suddenly and unexpectedly – car crashes, plane crashes, massive heart attacks, freak accidents – but then at least the final days of someone's life, even the final hour, could potentially be lived as happily as the years leading up to it. Rather than in a state of growing fear, anxiety and physical breakdown, which was what I felt like I kept seeing.

Joan and I had another performance talk, and for the first time since we started having these talks, I felt like she was not being unduly critical or crabby or jealous; she was being accurate. She was pointing out that this just probably wasn't the right field for me to be in. In the end, it didn't have to be that I would get fired for slacking off or for not taking it seriously enough or for being too stupid; I'd get fired for simply not being a good fit with the life sciences industry.

But I still felt terrified afterwards, because I knew that the consequences were dire if I lost my job. I was supporting a family of four and carrying our health insurance. If I lost my job, we'd immediately have to try to sell our house, which would be a miserable process whether we found a buyer or not. And then there was Rick's weight loss surgery scheduled for May. What if we lost our insurance before then?

Boston Globe – April 17, 2008
His heart says go: November attack won't keep Carlisle man out of Marathon
By Nancy Shohet West

Ronald Kmiec of Carlisle once said it would probably take a coma to prevent him from going out for his daily run.

Last Thanksgiving, it almost came true.

Kmiec had joined about 2,500 other runners at the Feaster Five Road Race in Andover. For Kmiec, a 5-mile course should have been a piece of cake; he typically ran 30 to 40 miles a week, and a month earlier had completed the Bay State Marathon in Lowell in a time of 4 hours and 3 minutes, which qualified him to run the Boston Marathon for the 35th time.

He hadn't missed a day of running in almost 32 years. The 65-year-old is a "streak runner" as defined by the US Running Streak Association, whose members are committed to covering at least one nonstop mile every day of the year.

Kmiec's streak began on Nov. 28, 1975. According to the official Streak Association registry, that makes him the streak-running record holder in Massachusetts, several years behind the nation's top streak runner, a California schoolteacher who will hit 40 years of daily running in July.

"As soon as the race started, I felt a pain in the center of my chest," Kmiec recalled about Thanksgiving Day. "It just stayed there."

After a visit with his mother and Thanksgiving dinner with his wife and son, he rested, and went out the next day for a mile. But the pain didn't subside – not that day nor when he ran the next two days.

On the Monday after Thanksgiving, he went to see a doctor, who recommended that he be transported by ambulance to the nearest hospital. He refused and went home for his daily run.

Then he packed a hospital bag – including his running shoes – and drove to Emerson Hospital. Tests confirmed that he had suffered a heart attack due to an arterial blockage, and he was transferred to Lahey Clinic in Burlington to have a stent inserted.

Awaiting the surgery the next day, Kmiec could not stop thinking about his running streak. It wasn't like there hadn't been challenges in keeping it alive. He had run with broken ribs and stitches, through hurricanes, lightning storms, and the Blizzard of '78, and on the days both his sons were born.

"I kept asking the nurses, wasn't there a treadmill somewhere in the hospital I could use?" he said. Normally, Kmiec eschews treadmills but, technically, a treadmill mile would have counted toward his streak.

"Your bed is alarmed," the cardiac nurse declared. "If you try to get up, the alarm will go off."

Sure it is, Kmiec thought to himself. When the nurse left the room, he got out of bed. The alarm went off. The nurse returned, laughing.

Kmiec had a stent put in, and for the first time in 32 years, almost to the day, he missed his run.

But Kmiec, a concert pianist and piano teacher by profession who comfortably refers to himself as "somewhat obsessive-compulsive," came to see it as a wake-up call.

He followed his doctor's orders over the next few weeks with rest, medication, and dietary modifications. He started a walking program. He enrolled in Emerson's Cardiac Rehabilitation Program. And with his doctor's permission, he started running again – on Dec. 28, his 33d wedding anniversary.

Having broken his daily streak, Kmiec set his sights on a record he was determined to maintain – his Boston Marathon streak. He has completed every Boston Marathon since 1974. Only eight other competitors have finished more consecutive Boston Marathons.

"Right away," he said, "I decided I was going to get back into training for the Marathon."

Ginny Dow, manager of Emerson Hospital's Cardiac Rehabilitation Program, said she found it fascinating to work with a patient as fit as Kmiec.

"Some of our program participants had very sedentary lifestyles before their heart attack," she said, but even trained athletes like Kmiec can be at risk.

"People ask how someone at a high fitness level can have a heart attack," she said. "But diet is just as important as a cause of heart disease.

Stress and genetics play a role as well. Athletes sometimes have a false sense of security."

Kmiec acknowledged that he paid little attention to nutrition, for exactly the reason Dow indicated: Being trim and fit made him feel inherently healthy. "I thought I could eat anything, so I did, much of it sweet and fat-filled."

Dow, who discussed Kmiec's situation with his permission, said he isn't her first cardiac patient who has run a marathon or achieved similarly impressive athletic feats.

"Working with us gives people who want to resume their exercising a greater level of security," she said. "When people feel symptoms but don't know whether to be concerned or not, we can check their cardiac monitors."

Kmiec's ongoing rehabilitation, like that of almost everyone at the cardiac rehab center, combines group support, nutrition counseling, calisthenics, strength training, and cardiovascular work.

Dow laughed as she described what happens when Kmiec gets on the treadmill. "Men are competitive with each other," she said. "The other guys in the program see what he's doing, and I can practically feel the adrenaline level going up around the room.

"I have to go around slowing the rest of them down, saying, 'He's running a seven-minute mile because that's what he was able to run before. Please don't try to keep up with him.'

So, on Monday, Kmiec will join more than 20,000 others at the starting line in

Hopkinton. In earlier days, he ran the Marathon in nearly 3 hours. "My average time is now 3:22 for Boston, and, of course, it goes up every year," he said ruefully. "I never expected I'd be running this slow."

Kmiec is hoping for a sunny, 60-degree day and a finish time no worse than last year's 4:26, when he was running with torn cartilage in his kneee in a cold, heavy rain.

He'll be wearing his heart monitor. And his cardiac rehab team has promised to be out there cheering for him along the route.

"I always envisioned that a day would come when I was in my 80s or 90s and would drop dead just after crossing the finish line of the Boston Marathon," he mused.

"Given what I now know to be the general condition of my heart and coronary arteries, I realize that if I were not a runner, what happened on Thanksgiving could have been a fatal occurrence. But now, all signs are good, and it looks like I can go on a few more decades."

Tim's running log: 4/18, 7 PM. Day 251. 1.2 miles. Cool but still sunny after dinner. Really nice weather for running, even late.

Every now and then, I felt the need to stop and acknowledge how fundamentally trivial our running streak was. Long before Tim and I were running, when I first wrote about streak-running for a *Boston Globe* article, I would tell people about the phenomenon – run at least a mile every day – and some would say "That's a really cool idea" but others would say "Well, so what? So someone can run every day – how is that a great accomplishment?" And it was often other runners who said this. It wasn't that they didn't think running was an impressive thing to do in itself; they just couldn't buy the value of the "every single day" part.

And so having racked up two hundred and fifty days, it seemed only fair for me to step back and admit it *was* a silly pursuit, the streak running. We were not going to save the world, not even one little tiny corner of it, by never missing a day of running. If we were going to commit to the self-discipline of doing something every day, there were better and worthier choices I could make. I could donate a dollar to UNICEF or Oxfam every day; I could reach out to someone in some kind of need every day; I could pick up ten pieces of roadside trash every day. I could find a way to be more environmentally conscientious every day. I could even resolve to start a streak to see how many days I could go without losing my temper with my children. Now *that* would be a streak worth boasting about.

But for Tim and me, it was a team effort; it was what we'd decided to put our collective weight behind. And simply because of the fact that it had forged a bond between us that did not previously exist – a bond of resolving together to do something that takes a bit of extra effort – it was worthwhile for me. Even if it contributed absolutely nothing worthy to the world whatsoever.

The morning after the talk with Joan, I woke up with a sense that something had been resolved in a very positive way in my mind as I slept. What had been resolved was this realization: This situation was *not* going to kill me. If I got fired, I got fired. I kept thinking of the lyrics from that Cat Stevens song, Moon Shadow: *If I ever lose my legs, I won't have to walk no more* – how he acknowledges that with every unimaginable loss would come in exchange a certain kind of paradoxical freedom.

I kept thinking, *And if I ever lose my job, I won't have to worry about company newsletter stories no more.* Meaning, if it happens, it happens; everything is bearable and everything has an upside.

As it was, I spent a great deal of every day doing mental calculations: *Joan wouldn't fire me today, because I haven't yet drafted the newsletter stories; but would she fire me as soon as they were written? Joan won't fire me in May because she has a vacation coming up and needs someone here to handle the administrivia; but will she fire me as soon as June 1 arrives?*

The other cultural reference I kept thinking of alongside Cat Stevens was from an interview my professional role model, Terry Gross, did with Julie Andrews on the National Public Radio show *Fresh Air*. Terry asked Julie if she was disappointed not to get the role of Eliza Doolittle in the film version of *My Fair Lady* after playing it on Broadway, and Julie said that of course she was disappointed but then said, "I *completely* understood why they gave it to Audrey Hepburn."

And in that wonderfully sincere British enunciation of hers, she sounded so unassailable – she wasn't just saying it, she really did *completely* understand. And that was oddly enough how I felt after Monday's talk with Joan: I *completely* understood why I might get fired. It was not that I was stupid or incompetent or had squandered a wonderful opportunity; it was that she wanted to be training someone who wanted to step into her shoes. She needed to be working with someone who was on an upward career trend. Not someone who was just grateful to be bringing home one thousand dollars a week. So, like Julie Andrews, I *completely* understood. I really did.

Tim's running log: 4/19, 6:15 AM. Day 252. 2.2 miles. We're in Pennsylvania so we went running with Lauren, Bob and Sophie in their neighborhood!

For Patriots' Day weekend, a holiday in New England and one of the few Monday holidays my company observes, the four of us drove to visit my sister Lauren's family in Swarthmore, Pennsylvania.

153

Much as I wanted to live mindfully and enjoy the weekend, I was so aware of the sense that anxiety seemed to be my new constant companion. I worried ceaselessly about performing my job; losing my job; telling Rick I'd lost my job; having to decide to sell our house; not being able to sell our house and facing foreclosure and bankruptcy.

I still couldn't trace back and say where we went wrong. Except that I should have been so much more financially astute in terms of thinking "I need to live in a house that I don't fear losing. And I also need to live in a house that it would be okay to leave – one that doesn't come wrapped in so many obligations to my family."

Yes, I'd gotten myself into this. Yes, I was pretty much willing to take the blame; and no, I didn't know the time or date to which I'd have to rewind the clock, if I had that power, in order to make it turn out right. I loved my house, I loved living on the farm, I loved our location near the town center, I loved living next to Mom and Dad. But it was also the thing in my life that caused me the most stress.

Tim's running log: 4/20, 8 AM. Day 253. 5 miles. Valley Forge National Park 5-mile race. Did it in 46 minutes!!! Youngest finisher. 655 out of 1,074 people.

The Valley Forge five-mile race was an amazingly eye-opening experience for me.

First of all, it was just fun. We were both so happy to be part of it. The weather was fine – cool at the outset, but humid enough that we warmed up as soon as we started – and the scenery was captivating: rolling hills, open fields, beech trees silhouetted against the sky.

The way it unfolded was a surprise to me, though. I wasn't sure Tim was even up to a challenging five-miler, given our short training distances, and I certainly never expected that I'd lose sight of him within the first two minutes. But that was just what happened.

154

"Remember, Tim, you don't have to stay with Mommy," Rick told him as we made the 40-minute drive from Swarthmore to Valley Forge. "You can break out on your own any time you want to."

"Rick, he's not going to break out on his own," I said, slightly exasperated at the implication that Tim had so much more potential in this race than I did. "We run at the same pace!"

Well, that had been true...during our daily runs in Carlisle. This turned out to be different, though. He started off at his usual tempo, just a little faster than mine, and I urged him to pace himself, but he just let the crowd carry him along and stayed at his own pace.

For a little while I could see him just a short distance ahead of me and kidded myself into believing that I was running back-up on purpose, to keep an eye on him, but soon I couldn't see him at all. Even on the long hairpin turns where you could see the line of runners unspooling about a quarter-mile ahead, I couldn't spot him. For the fifty-two minutes I ran, I had Tim in my sights for only about two of those; the rest of the time I had to go on faith that he was okay.

And therein lay another obvious but irresistible metaphor, this time not just about running but about racing. Although the race's enrollment was about one thousand, we were spread out enough that there were never more than about three abreast on the roadway. We weren't packed in, like the descriptions I'd heard of the Boston Marathon and some other tremendously popular races. So as I ran, I felt really apprehensive about losing sight of him so quickly, but I knew that if anything went really wrong for him – like a medical emergency or if he suddenly didn't want to run without me – I'd see him off to the side, and where he was so much younger than everyone else and there was a fair amount of race staff around, I knew if anything was wrong, someone would help him and would find me. So I knew nothing terrible would happen without my knowing.

At the same time, the five miles gave me plenty of time to feel anxious about just how he was doing. Was he comfortable with the run? Was he having any trouble? Were the people around him being friendly? Were they encouraging him? Did he feel isolated, in a crowd surrounded by strangers? Was he noticing the beautiful countryside? Did he regret the decision to go tearing off ahead of me?

And what about the water stops? Did he see how you could just reach out and be handed a cup of water, and then toss it to the side when you were done? Or, knowing Tim, was he reticent to try doing something he didn't know the exact protocol for?

As I was thinking about this, I couldn't help conceding to myself that this was exactly what it would be like when he went off to college, or the military, or whatever his first major break from home turned out to be: I'd assume that if anything was *really* wrong I'd find out, but for the most part I'd just have to have faith that he was happy and comfortable and getting along with the people around him, or that he'd figure out how to get help if he needed it.

When the race ended, I learned that Tim had run it in forty-six minutes and was ecstatic with the whole experience: proud of himself and delighted with how much fun he had. Frankly, we were both astonished by the fact that he finished seven minutes ahead of me. It put a different perspective on all our running, knowing how much faster he could actually go than I could – and knowing that it turned out not to matter a bit that we hadn't done the kind of training for the race that I thought we should.

Tim's running log: 4/21, 9 AM. Day 254. 2.6 miles. We are still in Swarthmore and we ran at the college track.

On the Sunday morning of the weekend in Pennsylvania, Rick took the kids swimming at Lauren's fitness center while I worked on my newsletter stories. Then I received an e-mail from Joan thoroughly criticizing my draft of the leadership summit letter, despite the fact that her edited version of it looked to me conspicuously like the one I'd written but with less prose.

I began to suspect that she'd gone off the deep end when it came to critiquing my work. Having my weekend ruined after two hours of effort on the newsletter with that nasty e-mail really made me throw my arms up in despair. I felt like saying, "Okay, I give up. We can't work together. I thought the worst outcome would be losing my job, but I no longer care. I can't go on with this much stress and anxiety and loss of self-esteem and overall misery. If I lose my job, I lose my job. It won't kill me. I just can't agonize over it anymore."

And as scary as that was to say, I started to feel different after that. The situation had bottomed out and something was telling me to just let it go. Just stop fighting it. If I lost my job, I lost my job: as Cat Stevens sang, I wouldn't have to write newsletter stories no more. If we lost the house, we lost the house; as Cat Stevens sang, I wouldn't have to dread conversations with Rick anymore for fear they would lead to him suggesting we sell the house. The stress and misery I was feeling over work no longer justified the necessity of work in my life.

If I did lose my job and Rick said "We have to list the house," then okay, we'd do that. We'd tried hard to keep it and we might just have to give up.

Or maybe not. Maybe something else was the answer. Maybe losing my job and being home for a while would free up Rick to seek out more clients, and maybe that plus freelance writing on my part would get us through the summer, and maybe then I'd get a new full-time job. I didn't know what would happen. What I did know was that I had to stop being so *scared*.

Tim's running log: 4/23, 7 PM. Day 256. 1.2 miles. Nice warm evening, almost like summer.

As I thought more about my performance in the race on Sunday, I grew a little bit discouraged. I knew that was ridiculous, since I was obviously not a competitive runner and had no delusions that at my age and general athletic ability I was going to impress anyone with my finish, but at the same time, I couldn't quite believe I'd finished in the bottom *fifteen percent* of one thousand runners. I just really didn't think of myself as quite that mediocre a runner. I knew I wasn't strong or fast, but I'd always thought of myself as steady.

The reality, as reflected in the race stats, somewhat changed my perspective on myself. It made me feel...frumpy. I'd been running for twenty-two years and finally got Tim interested; I had viewed myself as sort of a fitness role model for him. But now I was feeling more like a humorous footnote to his athletic ascent. He actually wrote an e-mail to his friend Cole about the race in which he said "My mom STUNK," and that didn't particularly bother me because semi-scandalous language in e-mails to each other was one way that he and his friends tested their boundaries, like cursing together. It was more just a matter of realizing that I made myself look like...kind of a loser. Not a fit and capable mom but a frumpy and semi-ridiculous mom, chugging along behind nine hundred other racers.

Nonetheless, I still felt good about running five miles and enjoying every step of it, and Tim was still talking about how much fun he had. Also, it motivated me to push myself a little harder in the week that followed, as I tried to make myself run just a little faster and stronger.

So maybe the lesson learned wasn't about getting older but about not getting complacent, about remembering that no matter what the activity, you can always make the effort to keep getting better at it.

Tim's running log: 4/24, 6 AM. Day 257. 1.3 miles. Trying harder to get up in the morning to run.

Seeing daylight when the alarm went off in the morning lifted my spirits. I kept thinking of Colonial women, pioneer women, and even before them the early Native American women, who lived on this land before we did. How much more sensitive to the change of seasons they must have been than I was. For them, the milder days and earlier sunlight literally meant survival, and hope.

Tim's running log: 4/25, 7:45 PM. Day 258. 1.4 miles. Cole is here for a sleepover so he ran with us.

Tim's friend Cole was yet another in a line of Tim's friends who were game to join us for a run if they happened to be at our house anyway. They were all good athletes – soccer, baseball, hockey – anyway, and approached a 1.5-mile run with a "How hard could it be?" attitude which I admired, and most definitely did not have at their age.

I let the two boys run shoulder to shoulder ahead of me while I tried to listen in on their conversation. What *do* nine-year-old boys talk about with each other, I wondered. First Tim described in blow-by-blow detail a boxing match that he and my father had recently. Then the two boys compared notes on their favorite miniature golf course ("So when you get to the pirate cove, do you take the uphill part or the downhill part?"). And then they howled together over some apparently hilarious play from their afternoon wiffle ball game at school. To me, it was beyond boring, and yet at the same time I couldn't stop listening. It was a secret conversation that had we not been running, I would not have had the opportunity to listen in on, and I was all ears for that mile-plus.

Tim's running log: 4/26, 3:30 PM. Day 259. 4.1 miles. My mom showed me a new running route, past a lot of marshes and streams, and also near Eric's house.

A vision formed in my mind of what seemed like the ideal outcome of my problems at work: if I received an offer somewhere

159

else, accepted it, and went to Joan to resign, and she then said, "You're doing so much better now. I don't want you to leave."

And I'd say, "But in terms of security, I have to. You keep threatening to fire me."

And then she'd say "No, that's changed; I like having you here. I'm not going to fire you. Just stay."

And I would.

Tim's running log: 4/28, 7 PM. Day 261. 1.2 miles. Down the driveway, over to the neighbors' house, over to Grandma & Buppa's, then home. Nothing too interesting.

Despite the fact that I'd taken advantage of so many wonderful conversational cues throughout our months of the streak – from talking about cremation while running in the cemetery to discussing the presidential campaign when we passed political yard signs – despite all of those invaluable and vital conversations, sometimes I still dropped the ball.

In late April, a two-year-old cow on our farm gave birth to her first calf. As we ran past the mother and baby, Tim said, "I'm really surprised that Daisy had a calf. She just did not seem to me like a cow who was going to have a baby."

"Did she not look pregnant?" I inquired.

"No, it's not that; she just didn't look like a cow who would have a baby," Tim repeated.

"Did you think she wasn't old enough?" I continued.

Tim again repeated his previous comment.

So, of course I should have taken the opportunity to explain that looking like "that kind of cow" has very little to do with it; the operative factor was that Daisy and the bull were in the same pasture last summer.

But I didn't. Once in a while, teaching moments just go by untaught. Let Tim's theory – that some cows look like mothers-to-be and others don't – go unexplored for the time being. We'd get to it eventually.

One evening I made a cheesecake. We were having a birthday party for the vice president of our division, and everyone at work knew I loved to bake, so I had offered to make something for the occasion. In fact, I've been chief birthday cake baker at every office in which I've ever worked.

This particular time, I was feeling a little like Amelia Bedelia, the hapless housekeeper from the children's picture books who makes mistake after mistake in her housecleaning job but always redeems herself by making a delicious dessert for her employers at the end. Each story in the series ends with Amelia Bedelia's boss opening his mouth to fire her and Amelia instead popping something delicious into it which stops him in his tracks. The parallels were unavoidable, from my perspective.

As I mixed the ingredients, the kids and I unexpectedly got into a discussion about my work situation. They were joking that if the cheesecake didn't come out very good I'd get fired, and then asked what would happen if I *did* get fired. Holly made the predictable comment about how then I'd be home more with them, and that gave me the chance to explain that if I got fired I'd be home more for a little bit, but I'd have to look for another job, so eventually it would be the same again as now even if for a few weeks we had more time together.

And then Holly asked me if I'd rather be home with them or working, and I told them that my first choice if money were no object would be to write articles during the day while they were at school and then be home to do things with them after school. But then I went on to explain that I need to make money for all the things we need, and if I didn't have my job, we wouldn't be able to live in our house, and sometimes it seems like that would be fine but other times we realize we really like it here.

161

It was a surprisingly fruitful conversation. Rick stayed neutral too; he did not jump on the bandwagon of "But we don't *have* to live here!" Really that had become somewhat irrelevant, our obligations to stay on the farm, that is; we had to live *somewhere*, and we had to earn some kind of income. So although living in a less expensive house would mean a lot less worry, it wouldn't mean that I didn't need to work.

GUEST RUNNERS AND THEIR HOMETOWNS 4/30/08
Cole H. - Carlisle, MA
Robert R. - Swarthmore, PA
Lauren S. - Swarthmore, PA
Nathan B. - Carlisle, MA
John M. - Washington, DC
John L. - Nashua, NH
Eric M. - Carlisle, MA
Nicole P. - Carlisle, MA
Austin P. - Carlisle, MA
Sophie R. - Swarthmore, PA
Alyssa A. - Sandwich, MA

DOGS
Tillie T. - Carlisle, MA
Angus P. - Carlisle, MA

STUFFED ANIMALS
Ba W. (a frog) - Carlisle, MA
Vicon W. (an elephant) - Carlisle, MA

Tim's running log: 5/1, 7:30 PM. Day 264. 1.2 miles. Again just didn't feel like doing much running.

There were two distinct ways in which the run-a-daily-mile-for-a-year project was not going the way I expected it would.

I initially didn't expect to get into the double digits. When we first tossed the idea around early in August, I thought we'd do a series of short streaks – three days; five days; a week – stopping for a few days between each restart. Maybe eventually get to twenty or twenty-five days, and then break for winter. I didn't expect we'd start on Day 1 and just keep going.

But the other surprise was those things that did not change as a result. When we set out on this undertaking, among my goals was to see Tim take a passionate interest in something other than video games and baseball. The baseball I didn't mind so much, but the truth was I didn't really mean take an interest *in addition to* video games – I meant *instead of* video games. And what was surprising to me, though it shouldn't have been, was that now he loved both: running *and* video games.

Which made me realize how absurd my initial hypothesis had been: that he'd say "Gee, Mom, you're right, running is great and video games are trash. Now that I've discovered the one, I surely don't need the other."

It was just another way in which I expected him to somehow turn into me. *I* like running and have no interest in electronic games; ergo, if he started to like running, surely it followed that he too would renounce the electronic games.

Well, of course not. And yet after almost nine months, it still caught me by surprise to see him come back from an energetic four-mile run on a breezy spring afternoon and start playing video hockey. For absolutely no logical reason whatsoever, I envisioned a dichotomy where none organically existed.

Yet another footnote in my ongoing education called He's Not the Same As You, otherwise known as Parenting.

Or Parenting Tim, anyway.

Tim's running log: 5/2, 4 PM. Day 265. 3.4 miles. Ran down Concord St. to Clark Farm and back. And we saw Mr. Kmiec, who was also out running!

For much of the winter, Tim had used our running time to tell me about various aspects of *Lord of the Rings,* which he had been immersed in for just about our entire streak up to mid-April, when he finished the final book in the series.

His distress over finishing the series inspired me to make kids and reading the topic of my newspaper column that month. It was like witnessing a bad breakup: since saying goodbye to *Lord of the Rings*, he hasn't been willing to so much as take a glance at any other book. I dubbed it biblio-bereavement.

Reality intruded, as it so often will: his teacher reminded the class that twenty minutes of reading per night is part of their daily assignment. So I took Tim to the library – for the third or fourth time since the end of *Lord of the Rings* – and this time insisted he find something he wanted to read.

He came home with, of all things, a biography of the band Aerosmith. It was written for kids, thank heavens, so I could assume the material was whitewashed just a bit. But for much of our run during the days he was reading that book, he told me all about the genesis of Aerosmith.

Hearing about Steven Tyler's youth was far more interesting to me than Mordor and the trees that could cast spells. Somehow the biography of Aerosmith seemed a little more closely related to my professional realm as a journalist than the history of Middle Earth.

Carlisle Mosquito – May 2, 2008
Read all about it
by Nancy Shohet West

I've been thinking a lot lately about reading: What we read, why we read it. Reading is something I've been doing for more than 35 years, so it might seem arbitrary that I'm giving it so much thought at this particular time. But questions about literary choices have risen to the surface of my consciousness with increasing frequency lately.

My five-year-old daughter Holly is becoming fairly proficient at sounding out words, but at this point she prefers to have chapter books read aloud rather than wading through picture books on her own. Last month, I started reading her a book I adored as a child: *All-of-a-Kind Family* by Sydney Taylor. When I told some friends about the book Holly was enjoying, they laughed at my description and commented, "The story of a large family of first-generation Orthodox Jews living in a tenement on the lower East Side of New York City. Holly must really be able to relate to that."

Well, I responded, maybe the appeal lies in discovering a reality so different from ours. But as we were reading that evening, I noticed something. True, it's about a family of five girls growing up in New York City on the eve of World War I. But in the first chapter, the big event is the girls' weekly trip to their local library. Holly and I had taken our weekly walk to the library that same morning. And although we had passed a cow pasture and a soccer field whereas the characters' route takes them past a pawn shop and a tin peddler's pushcart, we'd had essentially the same conversation as the girls in the book — about the fun of picking out books every week.

My son Tim is facing a different issue where reading is concerned. Late last summer, he began the *Lord of the Rings* series, starting with *The Hobbit* and proceeding through the three books that follow. He finished the final appendix of the final book a month ago — and hasn't wanted to read anything since, because in his mind, nothing could possibly compare to the joy of reading *The Lord of the Rings*. I try to woo him with other series – books clearly modeled on *The Lord of the Rings*, with craggy landscapes and glittering talismans on the cover – but he seems to want to wallow in literary bereavement for the time being. Once he moves past denial and toward acceptance, I plan to offer him Harry Potter, but for now, he's apparently not ready for a rebound-relationship read.

Meanwhile, my father, a retiree who taught high school English for 40 years, is connected to yet another kind of literary audience. As a volunteer, he leads a book discussion group at the Concord prison every week. After I finished the current best-seller *Water for Elephants*, I recommended that he consider it for his prison group. The plot of the novel involves a second-rate traveling circus in Depression-era America. His group has had far-ranging reactions about all kinds of works of literature, and he often comments that their discussions tend to be surprisingly similar to those he remembers from his four decades of teaching high school – the key difference being that unlike overscheduled suburban teens, the inmates never complain that they didn't have enough time to finish the book.

However, the prison has no budget for the book group, so Dad is somewhat limited to those books of which he can easily find a dozen or more used copies. At first it seemed unlikely that he'd be able to gather enough copies of a new release like *Water for Elephants*. But then I put the word out to two of my friends who love to read: Jenn, an editor; and Heidi, a teacher. Jenn gathered four copies from her extended family; Heidi drummed up ten more from her book group.

And as far as I know, not one of the people who were asked – not Jenn and Heidi, nor the relatives or book group members – hesitated at the idea of giving their books to inmates. No one questioned whether the prisoners were worthy enough recipients. People who love to read understand the immeasurable value of a good book – to convicts as well as to the rest of us. In fact, maybe to convicts even more.

I suppose I've known this for the 35 years I've been reading, but sometimes events conspire to show us things we probably knew all along. Books matter. Stories matter. They matter to a five-year-old in Carlisle learning about early 20th-century tenement life in New York. And to a third grader who can't quite bear to pick up another book while *The Lord of the Rings* is still coursing through his dreams. And not least of all, to a group of Carlisle women who recently passed along their books to a dozen convicted criminals, knowing that what we read transcends so many of the incidental facts and characteristics that serve to define us.

Tim's running log: 5/5, 7 PM. Day 268. 1.5 miles. Holly came with us! We didn't think she could run a mile, but she did! We went a half-mile out on the footpath and back, and then she went inside and then me and my mom did another half-mile.

Rick told me he'd run into Kate and she had a fairly good diagnosis: her cancer had not grown in the past little while. And that was good news, of course. But it made me wonder all over again how she managed, knowing what she knew: that something was taking over her body and that it might take her away from her children before they were old enough to lose her.

It's one thing to be optimistic for yourself, but how do you go on, knowing that your children will someday possibly soon have to learn to navigate their days without you there? I started thinking about my sisters and me, each of us with children at different stages, with a different kind of household and very different husbands: what if it happened to one of us? How would we put things into place for our eventual absence?

Tim's running log: 5/10, 5 PM. Day 273. 2.5 miles. I went swimming with Cole and my mom picked me up at his house so we went running in his neighborhood. It's nice and flat and easy.

May began with beautiful spring weather, bright green leaves sprouting and flower blossoms slowly unfurling. Spring came late, but magnificently. One afternoon Tim's friend Cole invited him to go swimming at their fitness center. That evening, I was planning to take Tim to a play, one I'd written a big *Boston Globe* story about earlier in the year. The performers were all middle schoolers who had dyslexia and were performing in a production written by two of their teachers about what it's like to live with a learning disability.

We didn't have much time to fit in a run between Tim's visit with Cole and the time we needed to leave for the play, but it was an experience that Ronald Kmiec had described to me and one that probably just about everyone on the U.S. Running Streak Association registry had experienced at some point: shoehorning in a run no matter how inconvenient.

Because I was interested in hearing more stories from streak runners, I contacted a runner named Joel Pearson from Washington state and asked him if Tim and I could phone-interview him. He was very obliging. Tim didn't ask any questions – like most boys, phone calls were hard for him – but I could tell he was listening intently. Joel was of particular interest to us because he started his streak at the same age as Tim. He told us a story about running a mile around the perimeter of an airport because he was stuck waiting for a flight and knew he wouldn't reach his destination in time to run.

I guessed, though I opted not to ask Joel this, that it happened pre-2001 – at this point it would surely be pretty hard to run the perimeter of an airport without being stopped six or seven times along the way by security guards – but it was still a typical story for a streak runner. Ronald Kmiec was once so sick his wife wouldn't let him out of bed to run – so he waited until she got up to feed their infant son and headed out for his mile at 11:45 p.m. I suspected Tim was secretly hoping for an adventurous 11:45 p.m. streak-maintaining run of our own before the year was out.

CHAPTER 10

May 13 – June 12, 2008

Several years ago, I read an essay by a woman who routinely walked herself through the drill of imagining her own death. She thought it would make her calmer and more relaxed when death actually came to her. She then described what happened when she was on an airplane that had to make an emergency landing. Believing the plane might well crash, she tested out her long-time practice, taking herself mentally through the drill she had long walked through in her imagination: preparing for death.

The plane did not crash, but she was convinced that the practice had succeeded in helping her stay calm. For this reason, I often try to mentally walk myself through events that, if they occur, will be traumatic. Several times that spring, I made myself imagine what it would be like to be fired: seeing our HR rep appear in my manager's office as a pro forma detail, the security guards going through my briefcase and then walking me sternly out of the building (the fact that our building didn't have security guards, and the fact that my co-worker Meredith and I had often joked about how lax security in our building actually was, didn't change my fantasy version at all).

I decided that what I'd want to do at that moment, driving out of the parking lot for the last time, was go for a long walk, preferably in a beautiful historic hilly neighborhood in Concord where I'd once taken a long walk after getting out early the day before Thanksgiving. Then, I thought, maybe I'd go to Starbucks and write in my journal for a while.

But for the walk, I'd need sneakers, and for the journaling I'd need paper. So I fell into the habit of keeping sneakers, athletic socks, and a pad of paper in my car. I thought of it my "getting-fired kit."

Tim's journal
May 13, 2008

Today was Primary Election Day in Carlisle so my mom and I ran to Town Hall so she could vote. And then we ran back after she was done voting. She voted for Hillary Clinton. I would have voted for Barack Obama if I were voting. We don't usually stop in the middle of a run but it didn't matter because it was 1.1 miles each way so we'd gotten our mile done before we stopped to vote.

My dad held everyone up in the parking lot because he drove up at the same time we were running and thought we would want a ride back so he was sitting in the middle of the road waiting for us. But we didn't want a ride, we wanted to run back.

On the way home, I showed my mom that my stuffed frog, Ba, was stuffed in my shorts. So he got to go along too.

Yesterday we passed the nine-month mark in our streak. In 90 days, we'll reach one year.

Though I always expect spring weather to set in as early as April, it's really not until mid-May that we can expect more than just the occasional mild sunny day. Work was so busy that I often went nine hours without leaving the building, and then felt guilty for failing to appreciate the beautiful weather we were having. Looking ahead to an evening run every day reassured me that I'd spend at least ten minutes enjoying the outdoors.

172

Even without the fear of getting fired, it seemed so clear to me that the problem with working, not just for me but for any full-time professional, was how much *time* it took up; what a significant percentage of a person's adult life. I didn't want to continue spending five days a week, fifty weeks a year, on the third floor of this office building – or any other. It just didn't seem to me like the best way to appreciate this magnificent world that we've been given.

But then I'd remind myself that things *would* change, simply because things always change. If we were to finally throw in the towel and move to a less expensive house, or if Rick took a salaried job…there were various ways that life could change and in one way or another, it would. It always does.

Tim's running log: 5/16, 6:15 AM. Day 279. 1.1 miles. Buppa is teaching me to box and while we were running I was thinking about boxing. Then my mom looked over and noticed my fists were curled up and I was doing jabs while I ran.

Catching Tim unconsciously rehearsing a boxing match in his head – and with his hands – while we ran one day reminded me of all the times I've planned out articles or essays in my head while running. Of course, the only problem with that is that composing prose while running is a little like writing when you're either drunk or dreaming: when you try to put it on paper afterwards, it's somehow never quite as brilliant or eloquent as it seemed in your mind. The endorphins somehow magnify the prose, and when it meets the cold reality of paper or screen, it's not quite the work of art that it was back when you were in your target zone at mile three.

So as I watched Tim, I wondered if it was the same with boxing. Do all the moves come out right when you imagine them while you're running? And then you find it's not quite that easy when you put on the gloves? Still, it was practice. Every article or essay that I imagine while running eventually meets paper, in one form or another.

Tim's running log: 5/17, 1 PM. Day 280. 1 mile. Had to go running alone because my mom was at a baby shower and forgot she wouldn't get home before I had to leave for Austin's sleepover.

It was just a minor logistical error on my part; I had to go to a baby shower for Rick's cousin and forgot I wouldn't be home before Tim had to leave for Austin's sleepover party. So Tim went running on his own, and then I went after I got home.

It was only the third or fourth time we'd had to run separately all year, and it underscored for me the fact that yet another reason that the streak worked for us and wouldn't for so many other households is that we were almost never separated. A man in town whom I know slightly and his teenage son did a very different kind of streak, but one that I felt a sense of kinship to: they resolved on January 1 of the previous year that the father would take a photo of the son every single day. They called it "Jumping Boy," because each photo featured the boy leaping on or off of something in a different setting.

Unlike Tim and me, they *had* to be together to execute their streak; it wasn't something either one could do without the other. I actually thought it was somewhat surprising that a sixteen-year-old and his father saw each other for at least five minutes, or however long it takes to take a picture, every single one of those 365 days. But it was another thing I feel lucky for. Unlike a lot of my friends, I almost never traveled for work, and Tim and I were both homebodies and liked to be around.

More importantly, we'd avoided so many other kinds of mandatory separations: hospitalizations, emergencies causing us to be separated. So all those times I felt remorseful for being away from my kids ten hours a day, five days a week, I should instead be remembering – and feeling fortunate – that hardly ever did a day go by when we didn't have at least an hour or two together. And I had the streak log to prove it.

Tim's running log: 5/19, 6 PM. Day 282. 1.1 miles. Holly insisted on coming with us but she didn't do very good. She ran less than a half mile and then stopped and walked home.

Joan went away for several days; while she was gone, I worried about whether I'd get fired once she returned. I was also wallowing in guilt that I didn't feel I could leave the office for either of two upcoming classroom events: Tim's class was putting on a play and Holly had an "author's tea," which is when each child reads a poem or story he or she has been working on.

I just didn't feel comfortable pulling the "Mom card" at work. And the resentment over that made me want to wail like a little kid, "It's no fair! I never get to do anything!", because I was so disappointed to be missing out on both events. At the same time, I wasn't willing to grovel to ask if I could miss work.

I tried hard to remind myself not to be so self-pitying: two years ago, all I wanted was a job. Two *months* ago all I wanted was assurance that I could keep the one I had, assurance which I still did not have. So I felt terrible about missing school events and self-pitying that I couldn't do what I wanted to do. I was deep within a well of frustration.

Tim's running log: 5/21, 7 PM. Day 284. 1.9 miles. Ran to the library and back so my mom could drop a book in the book slot.

Massachusetts Senator Ted Kennedy was diagnosed in late May with a malignant brain tumor. Once the shock of that initial discovery had died down, it was almost Memorial Day weekend, and the oversized headlines of numerous newspapers focused on the fact that he had checked out of the hospital against his doctors' recommendations because he wanted to return to Cape Cod to go sailing.

175

Although it seemed as if much of the coverage questioned his decision to check out of the hospital prematurely, it made so much sense to me. If you're seventy-six years old and find out you might very well die soon, do you stay in the hospital and talk about chemotherapy that might give you six more months than you would otherwise have, or do you go sailing in Nantucket Sound?

Sailing sounded so much more logical to me, and brave as well. I'd like to think if I received a grim sentence regarding my mortality, I'd have the courage to do something outdoors rather than stay in a hospital, as well.

Tim's running log: 5/22, 6 AM. Day 285. 1.1 miles. We went in the morning and it was nice out because the sun was already up, but I was still really tired.

Frequently, our morning runs would start with Tim in a terrible mood: tired, sulky, sullen. While I would have already been up for a half-hour, he essentially rolled out of bed and on out the door, pausing only to throw on a pair of shorts and tie his shoes. One morning he was going along in his usual funk when all of the sudden he surprised me by bursting into peals of laughter. He confessed that as we ran, he'd been silently composing a song about hobbits, which he then sang through two or three times. It was rather Winnie-the-Pooh-like, and not all that Tim-like.

That emphasized to me the extent to which this was truly a glass-half-full/glass-half-empty situation. One reason we embarked upon the streak project was that I wanted to see if it could help us get along better. What it seemed to have done was all-but-guarantee that we'd get along well for the duration of our run every day: ten to twenty minutes most of the time. Not to say we never got along well the rest of the time, but it was those minutes that were guaranteed.

So sometimes I felt like the experiment was a failure because other than when we were out on a run, we were generally *not* getting along notably better. And other times I felt like it was a success, because every single day we had a great time together for ten or twenty minutes.

> **Tim's running log: 5/23, 6 PM. Day 286. 1.4 miles. Today is my mom and dad's wedding anniversary! They have been married 16 years.**

Tim had to go to school an hour early one morning because of a field trip, so I dropped him off on my way to work. Sitting in the car watching him stride up the hill to the classroom building made me so regretful that I didn't get to be in on this part of the day more often. I so wished that instead of sitting in the car needing to get to work, I was again walking up to school with him on a daily basis, the way I did when he was in kindergarten and first grade.

Watching the kids march into school is such a joy, simultaneously trivial and profound. I almost never got to do that. Nor had I ever seen Holly get off the bus. I felt like I was missing out on so much, both by not being able to be part of their school life and by not getting to enjoy my own stay-at-home-mom days while they're in school. But then I so easily remembered the other side of it: how desperate I was for a job by the end of my stay-at-home-mom days, and more importantly, how other mothers never get to see their sons stride up to third grade and it's not because they have to be at work; it's because they're dead. Or institutionalized. Or serving military duty. I was lucky I could sit down to dinner with my children every night; I had no right to be bemoaning other losses.

> **Tim's running log: 5/26, 5 PM. Day 289. 2.2 miles. We had a really busy day because I had a baseball game and we helped some neighbors clean up their yard and then tonight we have a Memorial Day cookout, but we still ran down Rodgers Road (past Natalie's house) and back.**

Memorial Day found Tim in an uncharacteristically chatty mood as we ran, and it found me in an uncharacteristically crabby one. The humidity typical of New England summers was just starting to kick in, and I was uncomfortable. Tim didn't seem bothered at all.

It definitely taught me something about empathy. He kept prattling away about all kinds of things – which bat he had chosen in which inning at that morning's baseball game; which cow on our farm has a sweeter disposition than which other cow; questions about why Americans don't have English accents even though the first European colonists were from England – all reasonable topics, but because I was feeling hot and irritable, even though I tried to do my part to hold up the conversation, I just kept secretly wishing he'd stop being so verbose.

And then I realized what a mistake that was, because he so seldom *does* chatter away cheerfully like that – and that's exactly the advantage of our daily runs. It's when I get to hear everything that's on his mind. So it was a lesson for me in Mindful Living: a reminder to stop wishing this hot humid run was over and enjoy the conversation.

Tim's running log: 5/27, 7 PM. Day 290. 1.4 miles. A nice warm sunny spring evening!

My first day of work at the life sciences company was May 31, 2006: the Tuesday after Memorial Day weekend. Although there was no way this was anything more than a coincidence which no one but me could have possibly been aware of, it was that exact same day two years later – the Tuesday after Memorial Day weekend, 2008 – that I lost my job.

When it finally happened, it didn't transpire at all like I imagined. Joyce from HR was not called in as a witness, and there were no security escorts out the building. Nor did I pass out or have a heart attack. Joan simply said, "I just don't think it's working. I know you've been trying really hard, and you're a hard worker, and you're a good writer, but this just isn't going to work out."

But what I expected to be the worst day of my life…was not. Even as Joan was looking at her calendar to calculate my last day of work for me two weeks hence, what I was thinking about far more than financial ruin was all the surprise benefits to the unhappy turn of events. All the office projects that were now not my worry or my problem: the divisional newsletter template, another issue of the quarterly print magazine, the new-hire letters. And all the things I'd be able to do now that I didn't expect to do: Holly's Author's Tea; Tim's class play; my friend Liz's midmorning get-together in two weeks; picking up the kids on the last day of school. Even before I'd left Joan's office, feeling inexplicably carefree, the maxim "Challenge is the same word as opportunity" seemed to be resonating to my core.

Tim's running log: 5/28, 6:30 PM. Day 291. 2.2 miles. It was warm out again and while we ran I was jumping to see how many of the branches on the footpath I could reach.

And so, after two years of hard work and a few months of frantic worry, I was leaving my job. Reality hit in increments those first couple of days after I found out. As the shock wore off, I started thinking about how financially ruinous this was going to be: not just all our usual expenses with no paycheck but also an additional $1000 per month in insurance on COBRA. But I kept reminding myself, just because you lost *that* job does not mean you won't find *any* job. You *have* to find another job, so that you'll have health insurance and a regular paycheck.

I swung right into action, fueled by the momentum of feeling unexpectedly liberated from all the things I did not want to do. I told my editors at the *Globe* that I was available for more work: on-the-spot reporting, news stories. I made my resume searchable on several job websites. I started contacting headhunters and temp agencies. But at the edges of the anxiety was also the feeling that something new was going to happen and it just might not be a bad thing. It might be a new start.

> **Tim's running log: 5/29, 7:30 PM. Day 292. 1 mile. We ran to Grandma & Buppa's, then out to the road, then home. Just a short run.**

For the rest of the week after I got fired – the first of my two remaining salary-earning weeks – what was weird was how good I was feeling. I had a completely inappropriate sense of optimism, the sense that things were going to be okay and something good was going to come out of this change. I should have been worried about how to pay my mortgage, but instead I was just relieved that the company's corporate communication needs were not my problem anymore.

I started job-hunting right away, sending out e-mails to personal and professional contacts and trawling the job posting websites. Though logic told me I should be feeling terrified, I just keep seeing it as a new beginning, a chance to make a change that I needed to make.

Standing outside one evening, I felt a gusty wind blowing over me. Wind of any strength when I'm talking to the sky is always my sign that Spirit is right there reaching out to me, so I said, "I'm glad to be here on this magnificent planet. It doesn't matter exactly which four acres. No matter where I say goodnight from in the future, I promise I will try to stand outside my front door, or some door, and be thankful for another blessed and wonderful day."

And the wind blew harder, and I believed that Spirit was embracing me and applauding the sentiment, saying "Yes, you finally get it. Your life is wonderful and blessed no matter whether you get to stay in this house or not. Wherever you are, I will be there for you; and wherever you are, it is right for you to go outside at night to be thankful."

Inevitably, there were other days during that month that I woke and lay in bed, wreathed in anxiety. In that respect, it was no different from mornings throughout the past several months, and yet the difference was that previously, I had lain in bed wreathed with anxiety about the status of my job; now I was wreathed in anxiety about the *absence* of a job.

When I told people I'd lost my job, most of them said, "Oh, how awful. Oh, that sucks. I'm so sorry." And it was true but it's not what I wanted; I want more reactions like that of my co-worker, Lori, which was "You'll be fine. You'll land on your feet. It's definitely for the best."

Getting out from my job might have been for the best, but I just couldn't see how we were going to get through it financially if something didn't break through, either for Rick or me, soon.

The last day of May was a Saturday. Tim and I headed out for a five-mile run with Nicole that morning; the air was mild and slightly humid, and I was very pleased that we were embarking on some longer mileage. The sun was shining, Tim was in a good mood and all was well.

Almost two miles in, we heard a rumble of thunder and noticed that the sky was a very dark gray just ahead of us. Tim immediately opined that we should turn around. I said I thought we'd be okay. Nicole, exercising the most logic of the three of us, pointed out that it was clearly about to start raining and we'd get wet whether we forged ahead or turned back, so we kept going.

Within minutes, a steady rain was falling and the thunder was growing louder. As we turned onto Russell Street at about mile 2.5, lightning started flashing, accompanied by ear-splitting thunder. Soaked, we forged on, and then right near Tim's classmate Claire's house there was a lightning strike very close by and Tim started to cry.

I was scared too, even though logically lightning is not much of a threat in Carlisle because there are so many thick forests – you'd have to make a real effort to be at the top of a bare hill or in the middle of a field. Nicole said she wasn't afraid of lightning since there were so many trees around us, and I took courage from that, so we managed to convince Tim that there just wasn't any point in turning back.

In my mind, I kept thinking about how lightning storms are sort of like contractions in childbirth: you just have to tell yourself that the louder and closer the thunder and lightning, the sooner you'll be through the storm. There were one or two more really frightening thunder cracks and lightning flashes; at one point Tim grabbed my arm. He was just so scared and I felt so bad for getting him into it. "I want Daddy!" he sobbed: the quintessential Tim cry of fear.

But then around mile 3.5, we noticed that the rain was letting up. We were absolutely soaked, but rain was barely falling on us at all anymore. And then the sun started to come out. And then Rick pulled up next to us in the car and Tim just smiled and made it clear that he didn't plan to stop running, so Rick drove on home. ("Get the camera ready for our return!" Nicole perspicaciously called as he drove away.)

I was so proud of Tim. We were both so afraid, and I hid it but he didn't, but he persevered, and he discovered that if you run through the storm, the rain slows and stops and the sun comes out. I don't mean to say that running in a lightning storm is a worthwhile rite of passage – it's dangerous, and I'd never knowingly choose to do it – but we both learned something about courage that day. And we ran almost five miles.

GUEST RUNNERS AND THEIR HOMETOWNS 5/31/08

Holly W. - Carlisle, MA
Cole H. - Carlisle, MA
Robert R. - Swarthmore, PA
Lauren S. - Swarthmore, PA
Nathan B. - Carlisle, MA
John M. - Washington, DC
John L. - Nashua, NH
Eric M. - Carlisle, MA
Nicole P. - Carlisle, MA
Austin P. - Carlisle, MA
Sophie R. - Swarthmore, PA
Alyssa A. - Sandwich, MA

DOGS
Tillie T. - Carlisle, MA
Angus P. - Carlisle, MA

STUFFED ANIMALS
Ba W. (a frog) - Carlisle, MA
Vicon W. (an elephant) - Carlisle, MA

Tim's running log: 6/3, 7 PM. Day 297. 1.3 miles. Nice and sunny all day and in the evening. I wish it would get hotter, like summer.

As I continued looking for a new job, it surprised me to realize that I had felt a lot more hopeless when I was unhappily employed than after I got fired. My daily stream-of-consciousness continued to touch far more often on thoughts like "Thank heavens I never again have to try to understand mercury testing" than "What am I gonna do for income?"

Tim grew consistently chattier as the weather improved and the daylight lengthened. One evening as we ran, he told me about the playground activity in which he and several of his friends made up nicknames: all alliterations, such as "Tim the Terrible Tiger" or "Austin the Awesome Otter." Will was "Will the Righteous Wizard," according to Tim. I puzzled over that until Tim asked, "Righteous does start with W, doesn't it, Mom?" I kept thinking of the Seinfeld episode in which George tries to nickname himself T-Bone.

Another evening he talked about the book he was reading, *Prince Caspian,* and his description was actually pretty interesting to me. I liked how he could get so caught up in a fictional fantasy world, even if he'd be equally happy playing NFL football video games on his X-Box. It's not one or the other, I'd learned: allowing kids video games might not have been my choice, but it does not in fact make them reading-averse.

My sister read all the Narnia books when we were growing up. I tried many times but could never get caught up in them and always ended up putting them down after the first thirty pages or so. Tim had her penchant for fantasy fiction; I'd always been all about reality when it came to reading. So again, I was back to this: Finally, in running, we had found something we both liked.

Tim's running log: 6/4, 6:15 PM. Day 298. 1.4 miles. We went out right after dinner and ran to the Bedford Rd. crosswalk and back.

Approaching my last week of work, I felt like I was in a reverse honeymoon period. With the whole thing almost over, there was a bizarre kind of relief. With another week to go, I couldn't really throw myself into the job search yet, and could take comfort in the fact that I was still earning a salary and even had several freelance writing assignments lined up for the upcoming weeks, between the *Globe* and a few smaller publications for whom I occasionally wrote.

Mostly, I felt excited at the prospect of being with the kids for their last week of school. In that respect, the timing couldn't have been better. I could go to Holly's "authors' tea" *and* Tim's play *and* Tim's class picnic. And all because I'd lost my job.

The cows were a frequent conversation topic for us. All the animals on our farm are friendly, and they have free range over the property; only the perimeters are fenced, so we have plenty of contact with them. Tim liked to talk about their family configurations; who – in his opinion – got along well with whom; the calves' various stages of physical development; and so forth.

One morning he commented as we ran past a six-week-old calf named Brownie, "Mom, Brownie doesn't even know the meaning of race."

What a profound comment, I thought to myself: the notion that racism is irrelevant to all non-human species. Had Tim been hearing a lot about race lately with the final Democratic primaries clinching the nomination for Obama? (In fact, once he asked me why it was considered historic that Obama was a presidential nominee, and when I told him it was because of race, Tim didn't even seem to understand the concept of anyone believing that ethnicity had anything to do with presidential qualifications.)

After he said that Brownie the calf had no idea of the meaning of race, I had about ten seconds to mull over the wisdom of his insight when he followed it up with, "When I'm on my bike and I ride past her, I always say, 'Come on, Brownie, let's race!' But she never understands that that means she should start running after me."

Wisdom indeed. Oh well.

Although I had made only a very small number of close friends at work, I was friendly with a lot of casual acquaintances. When I thought of everyone I'd have to say goodbye to, it bothered me to note that with the exception of Meredith, they'd all been with the company longer than I had. They all greeted me as a new arrival exactly two years earlier; at that time, they were old hands already who welcomed me in. And now I had to go to them and admit that I couldn't cut it, that while they would continue on, happy and secure, I had been deemed *not worthy*.

And in the same vein, when all my little tasks were going well, as they did for much of that week – finishing stories, ordering print materials, setting up the weekly newsletter – then too, I felt resentful that I was deemed *not worthy*, because it seemed to me that I was doing just fine at all of my routine responsibilities, and at that point I realized how much Joan had to have wanted to get rid of me to take that step.

One afternoon, Rick called me at work to say "You know, I feel like good things are going to happen. I feel like your losing your job was the start of good things happening to us."

He had gotten a call from a recruiter, and talk of the weight loss surgery was back on even though it meant paying COBRA. We knew we should be worried, but it was like there was something, some karma, in the air, causing us to feel inexplicably optimistic, as if my losing my job booted us out of a rut and into something new, a phase with all kinds of potential.

Tim's running log: 6/7, 11 AM. Day 301. 4.2 miles. We're having hot weather finally and it's really nice for running. We went down to Cutter's Ridge and then all the way to Clark Farm and then home.

On weekday mornings, I often found myself faced with a dilemma. Due to Tim's baseball schedule, it was really important that we run early, since his evenings were booked with practices and games. Most days when I first woke him up, he was whimpery and miserable. And it was so important to me to make it *his* choice whether or not we ran: I never wanted to catch myself pressuring him.

At the same time, a nine-year-old boy just doesn't understand time management well enough to realize that if you have baseball all evening, 6 a.m. might be the only chance to go running. And yet I knew he'd be disappointed if night came and we hadn't gone. So sometimes I had to coax him out of bed despite my resolve to make it his decision, only because I knew that deep down it was what he wanted to do, and he just hadn't yet developed enough capacity for delayed gratitude to realize that accomplishing the goal of fitting in a daily run meant enduring the fleeting misery of getting up early.

Tim's running log: 6/9, 7:45 PM. Day 303. 1.8 miles. Up to the library and back. Saw Austin going in to do his research project.

Tim discovered the *Guinness Book of World Records*, which provided us with plenty of fodder for discussion as we ran. Like how old the world's oldest turtle was. And how long the longest rubber band was. He loved that stuff. And it made me laugh to hear him spout off random facts that he found fascinating.

The first heat wave of the season set in as the first week of June ended. It reminded me of the ways in which hot weather with young children is both fun and exhausting. There's so much that's fun to do in hot weather – pond-splashing, walking down the road to Kimballs for ice cream, finding a breeze and some shade – but it also makes one lapse so easily into weariness and crankiness.

On that hot Sunday morning, Holly asked if she could set up her wading pool and play in it for a little while. I said she could, and then sat out in a lawn chair next to the wading pool reading the Sunday *New York Times*.

We had planned to go to church, but Holly kept asking for "Just two more minutes" until I decided we really didn't need to go. It seemed obvious to me that Holly was making the correct choice. On a sweltering day, she was opting to stay and play in the wading pool rather than get dressed, get into the car, drive to church.

No, there was no question that what we were doing was more enjoyable. I knew there was not a thing better to be doing on that 95-degree June day than sitting in the shade, reading the paper, watching my daughter splash in the water.

Tim's running log: 6/10, 6 PM. Day 304. 1 mile. Still hot out. Very nice for running early in the morning. Now I'm not so tired when it's time to get up.

And then it was June 10th, two weeks to the day since I sat in Joan's office and she said, "You have two weeks." I remembered so many good times at work: mostly the surreal sense first thing in the morning when the stairwell would smell like a diner and I'd think "Another day at The Office, people bustling around; none of it is quite real to me but strangely enough I'm on their payroll." The times when Joan was delighted with my work, with my writing. The times I showed off my *Globe* articles. The many times I took a walk around that Waltham neighborhood during lunch.

I remembered bad times too. All the mistakes I'd made, and all the ones I caught at almost the last minute. All the times Joan castigated my work, mostly by e-mail: "You're missing the point, that's *not* what's important here." And all the closed-door sessions in her office over the past four months: "I have to tell you, Nancy, I just don't think this is working out. I know you're trying, but I'm just not sure you can do it. This might just not be the right match for you. I think you need to do some soul-searching. I know you're trying, but it's *just not working*."

And then it was my last day. I felt a little queasy about the idea of actually saying goodbye and walking out of the building, but I was also absurdly elated to think that after that day, no more responsibilities to this company or this job. Ever.

On my first day of unemployment, the kids and I biked to school: Tim on his own, of course, and Holly on the Tagalong bike attachment. After I returned from school, I had a phone interview for a marketing company that writes blogs for other companies, which felt like an auspicious start. Putting together a few contract opportunities like that one would mean I could justify working from home and being self-employed, while Rick took up the mantle of external employment. Which wasn't what he wanted to do, but as I kept telling myself, fair is fair. For several years, he'd had the privileges of self-employment while I went off to work every day. Fairness, forced into play by my job termination, seemed to dictate that it was time to reverse roles.

Boston Globe – June 22, 2008
So who wants a happy worker?
by Nancy Shohet West

For the past two years, writing for a biosciences company in Waltham was my "real" job, the corporate post that gave me the necessary benefits and financial stability so that I could spend my free time writing essays and articles. But my yearly performance review at work didn't go so well this year.

It wasn't that I hadn't reached last year's goals or fulfilled my assignments. The problem was with the "career objectives" section, which requires the employee to lay out the next steps in his or her desired career path. I couldn't seem to fill it in.

"But what do you want to *do* with your life?" my manager implored, sounding more like the parent of a wayward 16-year-old than an executive overseeing a professional department.

"I want to do *this*," I responded, increasingly frustrated as we scheduled meeting after meeting to try to resolve the problem. "I like every project I've worked on in the past year. I've established good methods for getting my work done, and I've put new practices into place that are helping our department. I want to do just what I'm doing."

That's not good enough, my manager said, though not in so many words. You have to have goals, dreams, aspirations. Appreciating what you have is not a valued attribute in the workplace.

It's that last point that rankles, because appreciating what I've been given is one of the fundamental principles on which I operate. Mindful living may not rank high with my company, but to me it's a core value. We all spend so much of our lives yearning. I've wished for a different physique, shinier hair, a cleaner house, a better vocabulary, more obedient children, more time to read. It may sound New Agey, but at my current station in life – middle-aged, with a very nice if not decadent lifestyle, healthy children, great friends, attentive spouse – I've come to believe in the fundamental value of feeling satisfied.

Not so in the corporate sector, as I learned during my annual review. Contentment equals complacency. Companies need growth, not stasis. To be happy with what you have is to stop reaching for more.

I suspect there's a complicated but specific formula that represents the ideal worker. To be too happy, as I was in my job, is a negative thing because it means you are no longer striving to improve the company's situation. On the other hand, an employee who becomes too discontent is likely to leave, or simply sink to a level of despair or indifference that can't possibly be improving the bottom line. The fine balance is an employee who loves the workplace but is just dissatisfied enough with the job to be always looking for ways to improve it.

So even though I could rationalize it on a philosophical level, I still couldn't repair my self-evaluation. When I tried to picture where I wanted to be in the 0-2 year range, I imagined myself perfectly content with the same job, at the same desk, going through a task list very similar to the one I'd just gone through. Of course, that's not to say there isn't room for change or improvement. I'm a writer; I'm always looking for a more engaging story than the last, a more cogent way of explaining a policy, a more illuminating description of a customer's needs.

But my imagination couldn't conjure up a whole different role for myself. I didn't want a big promotion or a corner office; that would just mean more hours at work and less time for my many interests outside of work. And yet in telling the truth about that, I was putting myself at risk of being terminated: for liking the job too much.

I surely could have scripted something that would have sounded appropriate, a career progression that would have set out a path of stepping stones to lead me ambitiously up the company ladder. But I just couldn't bring myself to do it. Contentment may not be one of the company's core values, but integrity is. I couldn't lie for the sake of filling in the square at the bottom of the evaluation form.

The point, I now understand, is to aspire. Mindful living is a wonderful attribute in the real world, but in the workplace, discontent is the fuel that powers change, and change is the route to greater market share. I had revealed myself to be a happy person, full of appreciation for the blessings that life has handed me thus far.

And that, in the corporate environment, just won't do.

CHAPTER 11

June 13 – July 12, 2008

Tim's summer baseball league began, which meant a lot of time watching games from the sidelines for Holly and me. I like summer baseball because the weather tends to be so pleasant for spectating: the games are held in the early evening, so even hot days have cooled off, and it's a chance to see the families we know from the kids' school whom we might otherwise not see much during summer vacation.

People were still asking me how my job was going; I grew accustomed to confessing with a rueful laugh that it had ended. That was usually interpreted as a layoff; I didn't bother to explain that no, it wasn't a layoff due to downsizing; it was a termination due to the perception of my boss that I was incompetent. A woman I barely knew commented to me in the middle of a game one evening, "We've been faced with layoffs at various times, and every time, it was the start of a new opportunity that we wouldn't have otherwise pursued." And in fact, that was exactly how I felt in mid-June: brimming with possibilities that wouldn't have otherwise existed. And if we couldn't make enough money to pay our mortgage, well, I figured rather sardonically, that was the case back when I was working, as well.

The streak itself notwithstanding, there are so many times when I question my judgment with the kids. Some of my friends hover so much more than I do, and so many of them have much stronger opinions about the right thing to do in any situation. I try to be intuitive, but so often a part of me is second-guessing myself: am I doing what seems right for the kids, or am I doing what's expedient for me?

I'm just not a hoverer. I'm not the type to have snacks on hand for every possible excursion, or sun block at the ready the minute the sun comes out. I don't have a ready-to-go opinion on vaccinations or computer use, like so many other moms I know do. I like to think I'm flexible, but deep down there's always the worry that I am in fact just wishy-washy. Or lazy.

On a hot afternoon as we were heading out for a three-mile run, Tim wanted a glass of seltzer, which is practically all he drinks. When he discovered we were out of seltzer, he announced he just wouldn't drink anything. Not a great idea on an eighty-degree humid afternoon, I opined. He said he did not care. I decided to let him learn the hard way that it doesn't make sense to get all obsessive over a beverage if you're going to be exercising in the heat.

So of course, he was thirsty on the run. And I knew what I had done in not insisting he have a drink was questionable, but actually, what else could I have done, other than refused to go on the run? If he wouldn't drink, he wouldn't drink.

I kept thinking of my friend Carole, who went into a very funny diatribe at a recent party about how overhyped the whole hydration issue is. According to Carole, our generation of parents is so obsessed with watering our kids, whereas she claimed that she played sports her entire childhood without ever seeing a water bottle anywhere near a playing field. And, she went on to say, as

194

with so many similar things we worry about, look how well we all survived despite not being reminded constantly to drink water.

On the other hand, there's always the fear that I'd cause real damage to my child with this attitude. Suppose he really did get dehydrated? Well, in this case, I didn't think he had. He complained a few times that he was thirsty, and toward the end of the run we looped through the parking lot of the ice cream stand so that he could use the drinking fountain. Then when we got home, he again refused a drink because we didn't have seltzer.

I pointed out that I wasn't planning to go grocery shopping for at least another eighteen hours, so he was only going to get thirstier. But then I felt we'd reached the point where I just had to leave it up to him to do the right thing. Which in that case was – *duh* – drink something.

Tim's running log: 6/14, 5:30 PM. Day 308. 3 miles. I wore my new ketchup bottle shirt and pretended to be a superhero named Mr. Ketchup Bottle.

As the last day of school approached, Holly kept asking if we could go to our local children's museum. For Holly, the museum's singular attraction is the art area, at which kids can use an unlimited array of supplies to make collages, sculptures and so on. Her frequent imploring that we find a time to go made me think about how much I really didn't want to spend the whole vacation telling the kids we couldn't afford this and we couldn't afford that, but the reality was that we would need to be careful.

Tim and Holly understood fiscal restraint, and they were generally sensitive about the need to spend money carefully. As I see it, it's okay for kids to understand that money is limited – something that my parents never discussed with me during my childhood; the first time I remember them ever talking about the expense of a particular item with me was when we were planning my wedding – but I didn't want my children to hear nothing but denials of everything they ask for. It was a challenge for me to find the right balance. Just as I needed to find a balance between doing things with them and getting work done. And a balance between keeping up with housework and not stressing about it.

I kept hoping that Rick's job search would turn up something fruitful, but he had reasons for not pursuing it full force. Having finally cleared the insurance company's hurdles, his top priority was scheduling his weight loss surgery, and he didn't believe that plan was compatible with simultaneously accepting a job.

And I agreed with him: it made sense to get the surgery done first and then pursue job possibilities. But I also worried that I was going to lose this round; while he held off, I'd be roped into another full-time work commitment instead.

Tim's running log: 6/15, 7 PM. Day 309. 1.8 miles. Spent the day at a minor league baseball game with Ryan and then went running after dinner.

A week after my job ended, it was the kids' last day of school, and therefore *my* last day of uninterrupted working at home. The previous week's heat wave had ended; the weather was crisp and dry. It was as if leaving my job took a huge weight off my shoulders and drew all the stifling air out of my spiritual room. Free of those responsibilities and, even more so, those grinding *worries* that had plagued me since February, my spirit felt full of clean, cool, fresh air – just like the real air outside my windows – and my day was full of hope.

At dinner following the final day of the school year, Rick and I discussed with the kids the outlook for the vacation, and I expressed that there were three areas of concern I wanted to address. The first was behavior, which I summarized as "fighting and whining." No using that threatening tone, and keep your hands to yourself, I told Tim. No *whining*, what more can I say, I told Holly. The second was household organization: children are to be dressed with teeth brushed and TV off by the time I finish my shower every morning, and bedrooms and the playroom are to be kept clutter-free, with bare floors.

The third point was my work schedule. I told them I didn't want to be working eight-hour days during their time off from school; but I also had a lot to do and it all brought in revenue, so what might they suggest? Tim came up with a reasonable plan, which was that I could work from breakfast to lunch every morning and then do things with them from lunchtime on. In the morning, according to his suggestion, they'd either play on their own, have friends over, or do things with Rick. I thought it sounded like a great approach, if we could pull it off. And I was happy we'd tried to do some problem-solving as a family.

Tim's running log: 6/16, 5:30 PM. Day 310. 1.4 miles. It's so nice to be done with school and be able to go running whenever we want (and do whatever else we want too!).

On his first day of school vacation, Tim asked if he could ride his bike to the library alone and stay there for an hour. I took a big leap of faith and decided he could. This felt like going out on a limb for two reasons. First, it was a matter of trusting that he'd be safe and that I wouldn't get in trouble with the librarians if I let him be alone at the library. But I kept remembering that the library, in fact that very *same* library, was the scene of *my* first forays into independence at around his age, and it just made sense to me to let him have this much-coveted opportunity, being on his own at the library.

The second reason was that my initial reaction when he asked was to say "No, because Holly will whine and fuss if you get to go and she doesn't," but then I realized, hey, he's four years older and sometimes he's going to have to be allowed to do things Holly is not, and she's going to have to learn that, and I'm going to have to endure the whining and fussing.

And indeed, that's what happened: Holly had a little tantrum, but I held firm: telling her repeatedly that it's okay for him to get a special privilege based on his age. She somehow survived her disappointment; I somehow survived her tantrum.

Tim's running log: 6/23, 5:30 PM. Day 317. 1.4 miles. Down to the end of Eric's street and back (but didn't see Eric because he's at camp).

The summer was off to a perfect start for me... if only paying the bills wasn't such a high priority. I'd wake up at six-thirty in the morning, work on a variety of writing projects until noon, and then have fun with the kids all afternoon. And in the evening, I didn't feel stressed about the next day. But I knew it couldn't continue for long, and it was strange to acknowledge to myself that someday I would look back on this as a brief happy interlude between the stress of my last six months at the biosciences company and...well, and I didn't know what. The stress of my first six months somewhere else? Foreclosure and bankruptcy?

As I told Tim when he remarked that it was fun having me around all the time, we didn't know how long it would last so we'd just have to enjoy it while it did. And of course, in that respect it was such an apt metaphor for life: isn't it always the case that we don't know how long it will last and we have to enjoy it while it does? With unemployment as with mortality, easy to say, harder to enact.

Tim's running log: 6/25, 3 PM. Day 319. 1 mile. Two days until the Old Home Day 5-mile race!

Carlisle celebrates Old Home Day on the last Saturday of June every year. The festivities kick off with a five-mile road race at seven o'clock in the morning, and Tim and I had sent in our registration forms weeks earlier. I was looking forward to doing another race with him, and finding out if he could do as well as he did in the Pennsylvania race.

As the day drew closer and the weather hotter, feeling draggy and admitted to Tim that I was starting that I'll finish the race in last place. Tim kindly and replied, "Oh, Mom, I'm pretty *sure* you will!"

I really didn't want that to be the case. Obviously I wasn't doing this running thing for speed; I'd always declared myself a slow runner – slow and steady. But I'd never considered myself the *slowest* runner. Given that there was no way I'd put in a time that impressed anyone, I didn't know why it mattered to me that I not come in last – we were talking about fewer than one hundred people for the Carlisle race, after all – but I just didn't want to be bringing up the rear.

For one thing, I was afraid if I saw that no one was behind me, I'd lose all my drive and barely be able to finish at all, even though I'd never had trouble completing a five-mile run before. The bottom line was that even though I knew I was not a great runner – even in a small-town race as part of the women forty-and-over category – I still wanted to be a contender, someone who at least looked competent at the sport. Just as with Valley Forge, I was counting on beating the few people who weren't really trying at all or who didn't even know if they *could* run five miles nonstop but showed up anyway to test themselves.

It was one thing to concede that *most* people run better than I do, but another to prove that *everyone* who tries, runs better than I do. ("If you can fog a mirror, you can beat Nancy in a five-mile race.") And yet I still couldn't justify to myself why it mattered. The closest I could come to an explanation was this: I've *always* said that it's good to do something you know you aren't the best at; it's good to do something just because you love it. But to do something you are admittedly the *worst* at...well, I wasn't so sure I could quite so effectively defend the point of that.

Tim had a great attitude regarding the Carlisle Old Home Day race where he himself was concerned. He knew that there were probably up to five kids in his age group of eleven and under who were likely to beat him in this race. Carlisle is just a very outdoorsy, athletic town, and there are some great adult runners whose kids were developing into strong competitors as well. Many of them just happened to be in the grade ahead of Tim. and he had no problem with that; he was just looking forward to putting in a good finish and, if possible, letting only two of those kids rather than all five beat him.

Tim's running log: 6/26, 4 PM. Day 320. 3 miles. One last practice before our next race: we ran to Clark Farm and back.

The day before Old Home Day, for the first time in my life I awoke with acute back pain, a twisting feeling in my lower back that made me gasp when I first sat up in bed. Rick has all kinds of back pain, along with all his other orthopedic problems, and so does my father, but this was entirely new to me.

Mostly I was afraid that it could be a symptom of something worse: pancreatic cancer or kidney cancer or kidney stones. When Tim and I started out for our run, I wanted to cry because it was so hard for me and I couldn't believe that after all we've run through in the preceding three hundred and twenty days, this was how it would end: me unable to go on due to back pain.

Moreover, every decision about seeking medical help had to be weighed against the COBRA dilemma: we were still in our post-employment grace period and would start paying $1,000 a month for COBRA coverage only when and if we decided we'd use it. There were less expensive forms of insurance, but if Rick were to get approved for the weight loss surgery, we'd need to stay on the plan we already had rather than change. So it was a matter of hedging our bets until we received a definite answer about his surgery.

Tim's running log: 6/28, 7 AM. Day 322. 5 miles. Old Home Day race!!!! I ran it in 42:17 and came in 47th. Also I was the youngest racer. But a bunch of 11-year-olds beat me for our age category.

Tim's prediction was wrong. Dosed up with Alleve to mitigate the back pain, I did *not* finish last in the Old Home Day race. I finished 63 out of 72, but beat my usual ten-minute mile. And it was just so enjoyable. Unlike at Valley Forge, I wasn't surprised when Tim took off and was soon out of sight, and in fact I was kind of happy to be running alone, since that was something I never got to do anymore. I also really like the Old Home Day course...Carlisle roads we travel down all the time on foot and by car and by bike, but different during the race because of the relatively early hour and, more importantly, with traffic closed off. A few people along Maple and East Street sat on their front porches to cheer us on, and it was a lovely, cool morning to be out running.

Tim seemed a little disappointed at the starting line to see not just a couple but a *pack* of five or six boys (and one girl) all a grade ahead of him in school, raring to go. He knew that most of those kids would beat him, and indeed, he came in sixth for the "11 and under" age group rather than the third or fourth he was probably dreaming of, but that was not a bad thing, from my perspective. He has plenty of chances to feel rare and special – even at the race, a couple of people asked him what day of his streak he was on – and it was good for him to have the opportunity to practice being not-the-best.

What was particularly odd for me to realize was that until Tim and I started entering races together, that Old Home Day five-miler was the only road race I'd ever run, and that was once, back in 1991. I remembered that I'd just gotten engaged, and one of the race officials congratulated me because she'd seen the announcement in the paper. How strange it would have been then to think *The next time I run this will be seventeen years from now with my nine-year-old son.*

Tim's running log: 7/1, 4 PM. Day 325. 1.4 miles. Now we're getting ready for another 5-mile race: the Fourth of July race in

Bath, Maine. My mom thinks she might come in last again! I think she might too!

We had plans to spend the holiday weekend at my parents' house in Maine, and I'd used CoolRunning.com to find a Fourth of July race for us to run, in nearby Bath. My friend Cindie and her family would be in the area for the weekend as well, and they said they'd come cheer for us.

The prospect of coming in at or near last place in yet another road race made me think maybe I'd found my calling: race caboose. Clean-up runner. As my friend Nancy reminded me, the Iditarod has the Red Lantern Award for the last-place finisher. The thing about it that nagged at me was that we wouldn't know a soul at the Bath race. It wasn't like running the Carlisle race in our own hometown, where everyone has the excuse that it's just fun to run with friends and neighbors no matter what kind of runner you are. My concern was that anyone who read the Bath results afterwards might see my listing and think, "So this person came all the way to Maine from Massachusetts to finish our race in *last* place?"

Tim's running log: 7/4, 8:30 AM. Day 330. 5 miles. Bath Road Race: Time: 41:42. Second place in the 14-and-under category!!! Won a trophy!

The Bath road race turned out to be a wonderful experience for both of us. The scenery was beautiful, first through the small, pretty, seaside city of Bath, then into the outskirts, and then along a quiet road that runs parallel to the harbor and has lovely little antique homes. All along the way, people stood outside cheering us on, which was fun.

Another aspect of the race that was new to us was that it involved a U-turn. The road out along the harbor is a dead end, and at the end of it stood a race monitor whom each participant had to loop around. What this meant was that the slower runners, like me, could see all the faster runners coming toward them after the faster runners completed the U-turn. So I got to see Tim along the way, which was unusual.

Mostly, I just tried to enjoy the harbor views and the scenic back roads of Bath without being too distracted by the loud breathing of runners coming up behind me and passing me. Another nice thing about the U-turn was that once I turned, I could also see how many runners were still following me. It wasn't a lot, but it was enough to reassure me that I wouldn't come in last, which mattered to me whether or not it should.

The end of the race was great, running back into the city with lots of cheering. Just before the finish line, I passed not only Rick, Holly and a sweaty beaming Tim but also my parents as well as my friend Cindie and her daughters on the sidelines.

With a time of 41:42, a minute faster than his Old Home Day race, Tim came in second in his age division of 14 & under and received a trophy during the awards ceremony. I didn't have to worry that he'd go home and brag; in light of his placing *sixth* in the 11 & under group at last weekend's race, he remarked, "I am *not* telling any of the kids in Carlisle about this race!" And I had a time in the 48's, so it was a personal best for me as well.

On our way home from the Maine weekend, we stopped to see Cindie's family in the coastal town of Georgetown. Their cottage is situated on tidal flats where there's a difference of a mile and a half between high and low tide. We arrived at low tide and could walk and walk on the packed wet sand out toward the horizon.

Cindie's husband taught Tim and Holly to locate clams with, of all things, toilet plungers. Holly didn't care so much about the clams but was just happy to be playing with her friend Rachel and Rachel's younger sister, but Tim was overjoyed to learn how to find clams. There was so little, from my perspective, that made that boy glow with happiness; when something did, it made my day.

And this was just such a case, for two reasons. First of all, it gave him such a sense of accomplishment; secondly, he loves to eat clams, so it was an accomplishment with a tangible reward. Once he learned how to plunge the sand for clams, he was unstoppable, so proud of himself and so engaged as he found one after another and filled a pail. Even when the rest of us tired in our clamming and just walked along the water talking, he kept stopping to dig and plunge some more.

Tim's running log: 7/7, 6 PM. Day 331. 1.8 miles. Really hot summer weather, but by the time we ran it was cooling off a little.

July days seem to pass slowly whether at home or at work. In the case of summer of 2008 in the West household, this was good news. It was such a paradox: being unemployed was such a big problem in my life on a macro level and yet it was so enjoyable from day to day. I'd go to the library with the kids; I'd do errands; I'd run into friends and neighbors; I'd work on writing projects. I was doing all the things I liked to do, having lost my job. I knew it couldn't go on – or if it did, we'd lose our house, which wouldn't be a happy thing – but I could not resist celebrating the fact that we were having a great time.

One evening I was cleaning up my home office and noticed that the drawers of my antique desk were locked, and I did not see the key anywhere. I always tell Holly I wish she wouldn't play with that key because eventually it's going to get lost, probably while the desk is locked, so I was exasperated that this seemed to be what had happened.

And then the next morning, just as I was sitting down to write, I looked over at the desk and spotted the key sticking out of the keyhole on the top left drawer. It felt symbolic: one of those moments when you realize that if you just slow down, open your eyes, and focus, you'll find exactly what you are looking for. It was in a perfectly reasonable and logical place; I just hadn't seen it earlier because I assumed it was under the clutter.

Slow down, open your eyes, focus. There it is.

> Tim's running log: 7/8, 9:45 PM. Day 332. 1 mile. Almost didn't make it out running today! I left my shoes in Ryan's car and my mom had to drive over and get them after our baseball game so it got really late. But we went anyway and it was nice and cool.

Every streak runner has a story about the day that almost got away without a run. Ours happened as we were approaching our eleven-month anniversary. It wasn't as dramatic as Ronald's 11:45 p.m. escape from his sickbed or Joel's laps around the airport, but it was definitely as close a call as I hoped to have before we reached our one-year goal.

Tim and I had both been busy all day and it was sunny and quite hot, so even though it was not logistically ideal, I suggested early in the day that we plan to run after his evening baseball game, and he agreed. That afternoon, he went over to his friend Ryan's house to go swimming. Ryan was on his baseball team too, so Tim brought his uniform and planned to change there and drive to the field with Ryan's family.

By the time we got home from the game at eight thirty, everyone needed dinner. At nine we were ready to go do a quick mile. I told Tim to go put on his running shoes.

"They're in the truck," he said. I offered to go out and get them.

"Wait, no, they're in *Ryan's* car," he realized. He had changed into cleats on the way to the field with Ryan's family.

Tim didn't have an extra pair of sneakers. "I just really don't know what to suggest," I said, stumped. Literally the only footwear Tim owned that he could possibly run in other than his sneakers were his winter boots, which he in fact did run in a few times when the snow and ice were particularly bad the previous winter. But it was eighty degrees out even an hour after sunset. Running in boots would feel awful, and quite likely cause blisters.

Absurd as it sounded, it seemed like the best option anyway. I told Tim we could pick up his running shoes tomorrow. Then Rick heard about the problem and said, "Ryan's family is leaving for vacation tomorrow." So I called Ryan's mother right away – 9:05 by then – and she said we were lucky to catch them because they had actually planned to leave that same night but were too tired.

So I drove across town and picked them up, drove back home, and Tim and I did our mile at 9:45. Which was actually far and away the most comfortable part of the day, and Tim had cooled off and rested following his baseball game (they won something like 12-5),and he was in a much more cheerful and chatty mood than he'd been in when I left the house. He spent the whole mile describing to me a play called a "pickle" that he and his teammate John had executed in the second inning.

Tim's running log: 7/10, 3 PM. Day 334. 1.9 miles. Ran through the Center past school. It's so strange to see my school during the summer when no one is there.

Several friends sent me a link to an article that ran in the *New York Times* Style section about two couples who (independent of each other) experimented with a marital-relations streak. A friend from high school wrote to me to raise the question of which I thought would be more difficult: their streak or ours. My first thought was that they were probably less affected by the ninety straight days of frigid temperatures, ice and snow that we experienced between December 1 and March 1 – or if anything, the wintry weather would have had a positive effect on their efforts. On the other hand, it's probably easier to put on your running clothes and go do a mile even when you don't particularly feel like it than take *off* your clothes and...well.

Tim's running log: 7/11, 6 PM. Day 336. 1.4 miles. Tired and hot when we started, but I actually felt better after a few minutes of running. The breeze cooled me off a little.

Even on the hottest days, Tim liked to chat while we ran, whereas I found it hard to keep up a conversation when I was working as hard as I could aerobically. One day we ran past a yard sale sign, and that inspired all kinds of questions from him. What kind of permission from the town do you need to have a yard sale? Do you need a permit to put signs on trees? If more than one household has a yard sale together, how do they divide up the proceeds?

Pondering this last question, he started making up a series of word problems along the lines of "If one household sells five things for ten dollars each, and another household sells twenty things for ten to fifty dollars each, and a third household sells just two things for twenty dollars each..."

If I could hardly think clearly sometimes while running, I definitely couldn't do math problems. But Tim could, and so he quizzed himself while I listened and tried to keep up.

Tim's running log: 7/12, 4 PM. Day 336. 3 miles. Only one more month until we reach a year!!

I couldn't quite believe that the way I was spending my summer – unemployed and loving every minute of it – wasn't exactly how it was meant to be for me. I was waking early so excited about the prospects of the day that instead of going back to sleep, I felt well-rested and ready to move ahead into the morning. Normally, if I wake earlier than I have to, it's because of stress and anxiety. But this was the opposite: the excitement with each dawning day sparked me out of bed in the morning. And that felt like an amazing way to be living. Even if it was only a brief interlude before I accepted the next 40-hour-a-week-plus-commute job that came along, it was still an amazing phase to be going through.

When we reached our eleven-month streak anniversary, Tim said I owed him eleven Almond Joys. It was astounding to me to think that we had one month to go to make it a year.

CHAPTER 12

July 13 – August 15, 2008

In mid-July, I received an offer to work part-time for a former student of my father's who had seen my byline in the *Globe*. She was a long-time municipal manager and was in the process of starting her own consulting firm.

We met for coffee to discuss ways I might be able to help her. I honestly had almost no idea what municipal management was, but I've learned over the course of my own career that almost any kind of company has writing and editorial needs as well as administrative needs, and what Michelle was offering me – 15-20 hours per week of paid work, most of which I could do from home and some of which would involve attending evening meetings in nearby towns – seemed almost too good to be true.

I know nothing about municipal management, I told my sister on the phone, but then again, I knew nothing about biosciences when I started working for my last company either.

Of course, that fact was essentially what got me fired. But maybe this time I'd get up to speed a little faster. Or fake it a little better.

Tim's running log: 7/13, 6:45 PM. Day 337. 2.2 miles. Cool air and nice breezes; we ran faster than usual. Even Mom did.

Even though the whole point of running together was to spend time together and talk, I occasionally indulged in a guilty pleasure: using my iPod to listen to podcasts while we ran. Tim brought his own iPod and listened to music sometimes as well, but generally when I chose to wear headphones he just ignored that fact and chattered along anyway. I kept the volume low enough that I could hear both – Tim chatting about favorite ice cream flavors while *This American Life* played via podcast – so it wasn't much different from being in the car with the kids and talking to them while listening to the radio at the same time.

Although I could rationalize it to myself, I suspected whenever I brought my iPod that at least one or two of the drivers who passed us were thinking, "What a disgrace: a mother who would rather listen to her iPod than talk with her son. What a terrible message she is sending, running with him while she has headphones in both ears."

But for me, that thought just reinforced the wrongness of judging situations based on a drive-by view. True, I felt a little bit sheepish about listening to my iPod while I was running with Tim. But the (hypothetical) passersby who thought the worst probably didn't realize that this was something we did *every single day* together...and that I really could listen to Tim with one ear and catch the headlines with the other...and that when Tim wanted to have a dialog while we ran, which was not all the time, I turned the volume off.

But it was also a lesson I tried to remember myself: It's problematic to judge people based on a drive-by view of what they're doing.

Tim's running log: 7/14, 5 PM. Day 338. 1.4 miles. The cows were watching us as we went by. They probably wonder why people go running.

Tim is one of those kids who can get frustrated to the point of tears if he asks me a question and I can't answer it to his satisfaction. One day while we were running, he asked me whether using a bicycle merits the energy that gets consumed in constructing it. I tried to explain that to answer that, you need metrics for comparison. That is, it depends whether you are using the bike instead of driving a car for your daily commute or just using it on weekends, and how often you ride instead of drive.

He would have none of it. He kept insisting, "I just mean, *is it worth manufacturing*, since manufacturing requires a lot of energy?" He simply refused to try to comprehend the "compared to what" part.

Another time, as we ran past the library, he asked me how my friend Angela was chosen as library director. I explained what I knew about hiring decisions: how they take into account education, experience, credentials. But if there are other candidates with equal qualifications, Tim demanded, *how do they decide whom to hire?* And nothing I said by way of explanation – references, interviews, personal chemistry – could sway him from the tenacious track of insisting that if candidates had equal qualifications, there could be *absolutely no way* to make the decision fairly.

So one evening during our run when he said "Mom, walking and running don't really do that much to fight global warming since the process of making the food we eat consumes a lot of energy. Like bacon...has to be smoked," I just didn't even want to point out that we'd eat the food even if we weren't walking or running, and therefore you need more of a basis of comparison. Yes, we'd had a lot of interesting talks during eleven months of running, but I'd also learned anew the meaning of *don't go there*.

Tim's running log: 7/16, 7:30 PM. Day 340. 1.7 miles. We did a new route, down a side street off Bedford Rd. It was nice and shady, plus we passed some horses.

Holly's birthday is August 3rd, so by mid-July it's always time to start planning her party. Meanwhile, Rick finally got a definite date for his surgery – September 10 – a month later than he'd hoped, but to my surprise he mobilized immediately on the job front, sending out several inquiries with the idea that he could work for the eight weeks before the surgery.

And for me, the challenge was finding enough hours at my desk. Between my new consulting gig and assignments for the *Globe*, I had plenty of work; I just needed to balance the kids' reasonable need for recreation and entertainment with my need for billable hours.

Working for Michelle was testing my skills anew as far as diligence and accuracy. Journalism was easy for me; I knew how to conduct an interview and write a lead. What was hard for me was detail work. In one of my earliest projects for Michelle, I noticed just before sending files to her that I had listed a publication date for an ad as occurring before its deadline. It was good to be reminded of the importance of being careful and meticulous. I still couldn't explain everything that evolved at my last job, and why I went from being a star employee to one who could not be trusted to work carefully and effectively, but I nonetheless learned from the experience. I was trying very hard to be a different kind of employee this time around.

Tim's running log: 7/18, 8:30 PM. Day 342. 1 mile. Thunderstorm approaching; we could see lightning far away. Too scary so we just did a mile and went home.

July of 2008 had an atypical number of thunderstorms; by mid-month, they were developing almost daily. After our adventure with the Memorial Day weekend lightning storm, Tim and I were wary; we had no desire to be out in the thunder and lightning again.

One thing I'd begun to realize about the running streak was that it had made me aware of weather in both good and bad ways. Back in the fall, when Tim had so often commented while we were out running on the heat or the sunrise or the nip in the air or the phase of the moon or the duration of a rainstorm, I thought it was a significant benefit of streak running that it made us so very aware of the weather and seasons at a level we definitely weren't before. Previous to the streak, I'd developed that negative working-person's habit of sometimes going from the car into the office and back to the car and into the house without ever exposing myself to the weather at all, especially during less pleasant times of year. One great aspect to the streak was that it compelled us to confront *every* kind of weather; we couldn't hide from the heat or the ice or rain or snow or whatever the day brought.

But the down side, which I became more aware of as the summer wore on, was that it made me judge every kind of weather in relation to whether and how much it impeded our running. I had always loved all kinds of weather: snowstorms... heat waves... frigid January air... thunderstorms. But feeling compelled to get out in any kind of weather to run made me a little less enthusiastic about some of the climate extremes we experienced. So it was sometimes a bit of an inner struggle to remind myself to still appreciate and enjoy all the different weather systems, even those that are not so appealing for running.

Tim's running log: 7/19, 4 PM. Day 343. 3 miles. Nice dry warm weather so we ran down to Clark Farm and back.

When I looked back over the winter and spring, I was both amazed and dismayed by how much time I spent worrying about losing my job. I thought it would be the end of the world. And then by midsummer, it was such a relief to be gone that I wouldn't have gone back for anything, not even financial security.

But at the same time, after I'd had six weeks or so to heal, it seemed normal to be probing the situation in my mind a little more inquisitively and critically, and particularly to try to discern why things spiraled into negative territory so rapidly. When I thought of all the conversations over the winter about things like why the weekly memo couldn't link into articles, I started questioning to what extent was I just not capable of the work, to what extent was I capable but just not willing to exert enough

213

effort, and to what extent did I let myself be intimidated to the point where nothing could go right? If Joan and I had stayed on really good terms, if the department had remained a sunshiny place, would I have still made all the same mistakes? Or was part of it that I eventually became so *flustered*?

I wish I knew. I had definitely learned that being organized and meticulous does not come naturally to me, and that was a good thing to know, especially before embarking on the job with Michelle. I just wondered if things could have gone differently – if I could have been nurtured differently, coached differently, and had a different outcome, or if I was just an accident waiting to happen, simply not cut out for that work.

I didn't know, but it did feel worthwhile and important to ask those questions. As Michelle's client list grew, it was clear that I was on the brink of undertaking another difficult, detail-oriented, demanding job, and so it made sense to do a lot of thinking about what went wrong and how to keep that from happening again.

Tim's running log: 7/21, 7:15 PM. Day 345. 1.4 miles. Another thunderstorm this afternoon, but it was over by dinnertime and when we went running it was really sunny and nice out. But there were a lot of big puddles.

In one of that month's many afternoon storms, ten people at a soccer field in Boston were struck by lightning. None was killed, but seven were hurt, some seriously. It codified for me that lightning was undeniably a potential danger. One meteorologist commenting on TV said that "If you can hear thunder, you are within the lightning strike zone and should stay inside."

Obviously we had not been following that rule of thumb a few nights earlier when we heard the first rumbles just as we were lacing up our shoes and I said, "Let's get going right away so we can be back before the storm moves closer."

I had been saying since February that if I knew we were going to have one of the longest, coldest, snowiest winters in recent history, I probably would have had second thoughts about

214

throwing out that mile-a-day challenge to Tim; I was starting to think the same thing about the summer of daily thunderstorms. All winter I'd thought once the weather warmed up we'd be home free; I never anticipated summer storms being such an impediment.

On the other hand, I still saw it as such an improbable stroke of good luck that Tim and I had both experienced such a personally healthy year. Neither of us was notably sick during the entire year of running. Nor did we have any injuries, other than the night Tim needed stitches last August. Nor did unexpected travel plans crop up, or car emergencies, or anything else that could have posed a pragmatic obstacle to fitting in our daily run. Weather, baseball games, last-minute *Globe* assignments, and social engagements notwithstanding, we'd had far more good luck than bad luck playing a part in our daily running efforts over the course of the year.

Tim's running log: 7/24, 1:30 PM. Day 348. 1.2 miles. We ran after a thunderstorm cleared, and just as we finished, we heard more thunder!

After almost a year of running, I had to admit to myself that the goal of leveling Tim's fluctuating moods hadn't really worked. Eleven months in, there were still days in which he was just as prone to brooding as he had been the previous summer, showing the very same behavior that had first driven me to suggest the streak.

That surprised me, though it probably shouldn't have. *How can you brood and sulk and be sullen when you're out running?*, I wondered rhetorically. *Doesn't outdoor physical exercise elevate* everyone's *mood?*

But it always came back to the same obvious fact: brooding wasn't an element of his *behavior* as much as it was a characteristic of his *disposition*. Tim was still Tim, and Tim tended to brood. The running was good for him, but as I observed to myself so many times throughout the year, it wasn't magic. It

215

helped, but it didn't solve. (Nor, as I'd also observed before, had running solved many of *my* flaws.)

One evening, I was looking at him as he once again pressed himself into the corner of the couch and brooded, and I was thinking "If only you'd go out and get some fresh air and exercise," and then remembered, *he already did.* Yes, it was a short workout – about 15 minutes – but it was a workout and fresh air nonetheless. And it helped. But it didn't solve everything.

Tim's running log: 7/25, 8 PM. Day 349. 1 mile. Did the common driveway route after baseball.

An unusual assignment landed in my lap from the *Globe.* A city-sponsored bike advocacy group based in Boston was organizing a Bike to Work event. At various locations throughout the suburbs, trained bike guides would escort groups of commuters to downtown Boston by bike.

My assignment was to ride with the northwest faction. It would be about a twenty-mile ride into Boston for me, and the challenge was anxiety-provoking. On the eve of the event, I worried all day. I worried that I wouldn't be able to keep up with the group. I worried that I wouldn't be able to find my way home from Boston – the rest of the group, including the guides, would be staying in the city for the day, since they were real commuters going to work. And I worried that I'd get hit by a car and never come home to my children again.

Kissing them goodnight, I had that ominous feeling I get when I know I'm leaving early enough in the morning and I won't see them before I go: What if I don't come home. I always think of the moms who left early on 9/11 for a business trip. *What if before the day ends, Daddy has to tell you that it turns out you won't see me again,* I fretted as I kissed them goodnight. What if.

But it turned out to be an adventure and such an interesting challenge, psychologically more than physically. On the way, I expended a lot of concentration trying to keep up with the group and also trying to figure out how to get around the necessity of riding home alone. Should I make my way from City Hall to the train station, which would drop me off six miles from home? I'd have to figure out how to load my bike onto the train, and I'd eventually have to find a way to pick up my car in Bedford where we'd begun.

Finally at some point I said to myself, "No, stop trying to get out of this. You're here to do this ride: embrace the challenge. Instead of trying to get out of the return trip, commit yourself to it. Think of how proud of yourself you will be when you've completed the whole thing. It will be an accomplishment. Just tell yourself you're going to *do* it rather than try to get *out* of it."

And I was in luck; a couple of people I struck up a conversation with during the ride to Boston said that after we reached City Hall, they needed to backtrack to their office in Cambridge anyway, and from there they could point me in the right direction. Having taken careful note of street names and landmarks on the way, I managed to get exactly to where I wanted to be with only a couple of very brief wrong turns. By the time I was back on the Minuteman Bikeway, I was tired and my back hurt, but I was also just really pleased that I'd done it all and was nearly finished. And it was a great way to start the day. I kept thinking, "Normally I'd be in work now. This is so different from being in work."

Tim's running log: 7/26, 8:30 AM. Day 350. 3 miles. Ran with Nicole to Cutters Ridge. She and my mom talked the whole time so I listened to some music my dad downloaded for me.

My worry when it came to my new consulting job wasn't so much retaining the employment – I very much wanted to, but my existence wasn't bound up in it the way it was with my corporate communications job – but rather believing I could do the work, because I'd feel so stupid if I couldn't. If I was too incompetent to hold down my job with the life sciences company, and too incompetent to hold down *this* job, where did that leave

217

me? Um, incompetent. Able to write community briefs and feature stories for the *Globe*, which isn't a bad capability but is a pretty limited and specific one.

Michelle sent me constant questions and reminders, and I understood it was a learning curve – learning the job, learning to do things her way, and simply helping to get the business as well as myself started – but I couldn't help finding it disheartening when there were so very many "What about this" and "Did you think about that." It was a busy and complicated job, and my guess was that Joan would have said it wasn't the right job for me: too detail-oriented. But then what *was* the right job for me?

I ordered myself to stop panicking. *It's been only two weeks. Give it more time, stay on your toes, work hard, and see what you can do,* I told myself.

Tim's running log: 7/31, 2 PM. Day 355. 1 mile. Ran in the middle of the afternoon because I'm going to Maine with Grandma and Buppa and we're leaving later today. It was hot and humid.

As July ended, my parents took Tim and Holly for a two-day trip to Maine to attend the Rockport Lobster Festival. It brought to mind a very specific memory from September of 1998, just days after Tim's birth. My sister Lauren called us from Pennsylvania to see how things were going, and then she mentioned that she and Sophie, who was then six years old, were going camping for a couple of days. I remember thinking, "Maybe someday Tim and I will go away for a couple of days. Maybe someday he'll even go away for a couple of days *without* me."

It was unimaginable at the time; I was in the throes of postpartum chaos. I couldn't even put him down in a crib; he would sleep only if held against my chest. So the thought of us spending two days apart was outrageously impossible

And yet here I was, almost ten years later, alone in the house. But happily, just for a couple of days, not empty-nested or anything extreme. It was a good feeling.

With Tim away for the weekend, I went running by myself. It felt much easier than running with Tim, which I couldn't explain. It wasn't that I altered my pace for him, though he frequently reminded me that *he* slowed down for *my* sake when we ran together, and there was no logical reason that I should find running more cumbersome with him, but heading out by myself reminded me of the way running used to feel. Light and easy.

At the same time, I missed having Tim along. Running with him throughout the year had not only been fun and interesting but also given me such a sense of accomplishment, a different kind of accomplishment from just running long distances or putting in a good race time. Once again, running was a metaphor for life as a parent. It's all easier and lighter when you're on your own, but more intrinsically rewarding with kids.

The night before Holly's birthday, I thought a lot about when she was born: that long afternoon on August 2, when my friend Nancy and her two-year-old daughter Katherine came over to splash in the pond with Tim and me. Nancy's due date for her second child was just two weeks after my due date, and Nancy and I were so happy to be able to spend the whole afternoon just lounging by the pond talking while Tim and Katherine played.

When Nancy was ready to leave, I stood up for what felt like the first time in hours and thought to myself, "Hmm, I'm actually not feeling very good."

Three hours later, Mom and Dad took Tim out for dinner at his favorite Chinese restaurant while Rick and I walked to the ice cream stand next door for a cone; when we got back home, I took a shower and then we left for the hospital.

At the nurses' urging, I used the hospital's new Jacuzzi while Rick kept an eye on the Red Sox game playing on a small TV that hung in the corner of the ceiling. Later, in harder labor, I tried to walk through the contractions; the flooring at the hospital caught Rick's attention because we were still in the interior construction stages with our house at the time, and I was irritable when he asked my opinion of the floor paneling.

It was a harder labor than with Tim, but then finally, Holly slid on out. And there she was: my baby, lying in my arms, crying upon entry to the world but soothed as soon as I held her. And then a wonderful long two days followed, more time than I even needed to relax in the hospital; I read two books, wrote a lot in my journal, browsed through all the new-baby magazines from the hospital's freebies bag, held Holly a lot, and finally headed home. It was such a memorable time, and so much easier for me than Tim's first few days even though that part is never easy.

I remembered the first time I tried to go for a walk without Holly, the day after taking her home from the hospital. Leaving her with Rick, I got as far as the driveway and could hear her crying and headed back. I remember how hard the nights were, sitting on the couch in the playroom all night when she wouldn't sleep, and then how grateful I felt when, at four weeks old, she suddenly started sleeping for six-hour stretches.

She was so different from Tim, every step of the way. Both of the kids bring me so much joy, both in their own ways: Tim for his intrigue, a mystery I'm always striving to understand better; Holly for her straightforward sweetness.

Tim's running log: 8/3, 4 PM. Day 358. 3.6 miles. We ran to Mr. Kmiec's house (to pick up my Old Home Day ribbon) and then ran back.

On Holly's birthday, I kept looking at her and thinking, "Six years ago today, she was a tiny and utterly dependent and

220

needy little being...now she's playing with her friends and romping around and doing everything on her own." She loved me but no longer relied on me for survival; she needed me emotionally but she could hold her own as well. It was really a wonderful phase to have reached.

Holly's birthday party went very well; after nearly a decade of parenting, I'd become fairly proficient at pulling off a backyard kids' party, though no one would ever mistake me for a professional party planner. My friend Molly's twin thirteen-year-old daughters came over to help, and that was wonderful, because not only did they do tasks but as the party wore on, they played so well with the kids.

And all in all, it was a good party. There were about twenty minutes when I worried, when it became clear that with forty minutes left before pickup time, most of the girls had already burned their way through all the organized activities, but that was when they found their way to the swing set, and then after that I started getting ready for cake, and the cake ceremony broke up the action in a good way because after that they were all ready to play again. Moreover, letting Holly open her presents during the party – always a decision to be carefully weighed – turned out to be a much better plan than I'd anticipated: not only did it bring all the kids together and engage them happily, but also, after receiving two stuffed animals, Holly somehow got the idea to go up to her room and get several more, and then some of the kids played a stuffed animal game for the rest of the party.

So it all worked out just fine. And I was very happy that it was behind me for another year, as I always am when the kids' birthday parties end.

Tim's running log: 8/5, 5 PM. Day 360. 1.1 miles. We are really close to the one-year mark. On August 12th it will be a year since we started running, but the real anniversary of our streak is August 15th since that's the date I first ran a mile.

Despite all our financial anxieties, there were moments during every day when I would look around and find myself thinking, *Every day we spend here is a gift and a treasure. Every day in the house; every day on this farm; every day in this community; every day on this planet. Rather than focusing on fear of leaving – whether the house or the town or the planet – it is so important to focus on gratitude for time spent here. No, we might not get to stay. That's not news; it's been true forever. Every moment we have here is something to be thankful for.*

Tim's running log: 8/6, 5:30 PM. Day 361. 1.5 miles. I didn't feel like running when my mom wanted to go, but I did anyway and it turned into a good run. Cool and drizzly out. We ran up to the soccer fields and did a couple of laps there.

Back in June, friends of ours in Carlisle had invited us to visit them at their vacation house on a lake in western New York, where they spend the whole summer. At the time, the ten-hour drive sounded like too big a deterrent to me, but in the weeks that followed, Rick and I began to acknowledge that we wouldn't be planning any other vacations that summer, other than weekends in Maine, so maybe a free invitation to someone's guest house was just the right thing for this year.

In light of the ten-hour drive, Rick suggested we leave at three in the morning, and somehow we pulled it off: woke the kids, bundled them into the car, and hit the Mass Pike before dawn. We were approaching Buffalo seven hours later and arrived at our friends' house just as they were setting up for lunch.

Patricia and Tom have a son in Tim's grade and a son in Holly's grade. Their vacation house is on Lake Chautauqua, and as Rick explained to Tim on the way up, "They have *all* the toys!" Speedboat, jet skis, kayaks, paddle boats, rafts, fishing equipment. For most of those four days, Patricia and I relaxed on deck chairs by the waterfront while the fathers and the children indulged in all kinds of water sports. I read three months' worth of *New York Times Magazines* and *Book Reviews*. In the late afternoons we'd watch the Olympics broadcast from Beijing, and at night all of us would watch kids' movies together.

Every evening Patricia would make a big salad and I would steam or sauté some vegetables, and then we'd throw a variety of meats on the grill and eat on the porch. From my perspective, it was like a vacation in a magazine. Tim and I went running every day on the quiet roads that connected the waterfront cottages, or at a nearby track where the other kids could ride bikes and Patricia could power-walk.

Tim's running log: 8/9, 4 PM. Day 364. 1.3 miles. We're staying with Anthony's family at their vacation house so we ran on a road that goes around the lake.

Our last day at Lake Chautauqua was cool and cloudy, and we went to an old-fashioned amusement park. I expected Holly to stay close to me while the boys went on rides, but I was wrong about that. She began at Tim's side on the bumper cars and didn't turn down a single ride from that moment on: roller coasters, spinning teacups, up-and-down airplanes. When the kids reached the miniature golf fairway, she was the first in line for her golf club. It was a reminder to me not to underestimate her spunk. Just because *I*, as a six-year-old, wouldn't have opted for roller coasters and bumper cars – especially in a group of boys – didn't mean it wasn't what *she* would want to do.

Tim's running log: 8/11, 2 PM. Day 366. 2.8 miles. We are at Niagara Falls so we ran on a path around a big park called Goat Island. It is the last day of our first year of running!!!

On our way home from Chautauqua, we stopped for a visit to Niagara Falls. The four of us rode the *Maid of the Mist* tour boat and had a big lunch; then Holly and Rick sat in the sun while Tim and I went for a run around the circumference of Goat Island. That day, we celebrated finishing our first year of running, but the official anniversary date of our streak was August 15th, going by USRSA guidelines, since it was on August 15th that Tim first completed a mile.

Back at home, I told Tim that I was promoting him to Captain of the Mother-Son Running Streak Club. I said he would now be responsible for time and place of our run every day. I'd still go with him any time he wanted, but I was no longer going to be the planner. Moms do enough planning, in my opinion: every meal, every get-together, every household task, every family excursion. Tim could be in charge of scheduling our running, I decided.

He rose to the occasion right away, announcing to me that we would run at five-thirty to the Bedford Road crosswalk and back. Naturally – since I was still the captain of the rest of our activities and hadn't managed to overcome my punctuality problem yet – we weren't ready at five-thirty; we were still returning from a swim. But we did head out at six, and we did do the run Tim prescribed.

During our run that day, Tim said, "Mom, I might have told you this before, but did you know that while our alphabet has 26 letters, the Chinese alphabet has over a thousand characters?" Yet another entry on the long list of subjects we'd discussed while running.

Tim's running log: 8/15, 10 AM. Day 370. 1.8 miles. WE MADE IT!!! One year of running! Now we can be listed on the streak registry! Mr. Kmiec came running with us and we did the School Loop, the same route as the one we started our streak with.

On August 15th, Tim and I celebrated our streak-running anniversary. Lauren's family had just arrived for a visit and gave us t-shirts they'd made that said "August 15, 2007 –???" Ronald Kmiec joined us for our one-year run, and his wife took pictures from the driveway. At the one-mile mark, Tim grabbed me in a bear hug even as we continued jogging along. His face was one big grin. He couldn't believe we'd done it. I couldn't either.

When our year of streak running drew to a close, I kept thinking back to one day during our stay in Lake Chautauqua.

On that day, Tim and I had started a run together and then I continued on my own after he'd done his 1.2 miles. The weather was cool and misty that afternoon, and I didn't expect to enjoy the run. But at some point it occurred to me that the cool, misty, cloudy air felt good on my lungs. No sooner did I have this thought than I said to myself, "But yesterday was warm, and I love warm-weather running. Even though I didn't actually have a very good run yesterday."

And that was when it struck me that maybe the biggest thing I'd learned in a year of running days was this: a lot of what I thought I knew about myself might be wrong.

Maybe it's because I'm out of touch with myself in some ways, and maybe because things about me change and I'm not always aware of it. But at that moment, I realized that maybe I was wrong in always thinking of myself as someone who loved hot-weather running; the hot weather had been wearing me down recently and I'd been wondering why I wasn't enjoying the running more, and yet at the same time I was noticing how good temperatures in the low sixties with mist or even drizzle in the air felt.

So then I started mentally listing all the other things about myself that I'd found I was wrong about over the course of that year. I thought I ran a ten-minute mile; I run more like an eleven-minute mile, except in road races when I really push it. Furthermore, I had thought of myself as someone who did not like road races, and yet they had provided some of the high points of the year. I always said the idea of running on a schedule in a crowd was the opposite of what I like about running, and yet it turned out I had fun being part of a crowd.

I thought I didn't like winter running, and yet winter – at least in the sense of cold air – turned out not to be that much of an obstacle throughout that year. It was the ice that had nearly defeated us, not the cold.

I thought I loved hot-weather running, but the hot-weather runs had become been hard for me.

I thought I loved long distances, and really I do, but distances proved more of a challenge for me than I would have expected.

I thought I was only getting better and better at running, despite the presumed counter-effects of aging, but indeed, I'm dropping off a bit now that I'm past forty.

I thought the point of running for me was to have a brief daily escape from my family; but that year running had been all about being *with* my family, at least one member of it.

I thought I wasn't afraid of thunderstorms, but it turns out I am; and I'd even managed to develop a new fear: twisters.

I thought I couldn't run before dawn, after dark, right after dinner, and on and on. I was simply incorrect in so many of my assumptions about myself. Maybe that was the greatest lesson of the streak-year. I didn't think I was someone who could run a mile or more every single day of the year. But I was wrong about that.

So, of course, a fair question as I look back might be what else I think I know about myself that I'm wrong about. I think I'm a fairly unimpressive parent, maybe a B minus, because I get impatient so easily and don't always have the best attitude about doing things with the kids. But maybe I'm wrong; when I look at the children I've produced, I think I might be better at it than I give myself credit for. Maybe that's what the streak-year taught me: you might never know as much about yourself as you thought.

And what I learned about Tim presented a turning point for me. I really love getting out there for a long, luxurious ramble to enjoy the weather and the solitude and the scenery. Tim, on the other hand, liked being "the kid who runs a mile every day." He wasn't invigorated by the scenery or the solitude: he liked building his speed, pushing his body and being known for his daily mile.

226

I started this project looking for something we could work on together, and we did, but the results were entirely different for the two of us. We got very different things out of running. In the end, it wasn't about making him be more like me; it was about finding something new for him to develop in himself.

So this was something we started together but now might end by branching off and continuing each in our own way. That wasn't what I envisioned, but it had turned out fine. Which was true of just about every element of my life so far, and for all I knew, it might forever continue to be that way. And that too was fine.

Carlisle Mosquito – August 29, 2008
A year of running – a mother-son experiment
by Nancy Shohet West

We ran before dawn and we ran after nightfall. We ran on hot August afternoons, brisk April mornings, and a January evening with a wind chill of 7 below. We ran in Carlisle, Concord, Acton, Bedford, Chelmsford and Stow as well as Maine, New Hampshire, New York and Pennsylvania. We ran in heat waves, snowstorms, the remnants of Tropical Storm Noel, gorgeous autumn sunshine, late summer humidity, and thunderstorms. We passed deer, cows, horses, sheep, geese and snowmen. We ran at Niagara Falls and Valley Forge National Park. We ran separately five times and together all the other days. A couple of times, when the ice posed a nearly impassable barrier, we ran in snow boots. We did four two races. We ran with friends, siblings, cousins, three dogs and two stuffed animals. We ran for 366 days.

As I've said several times since my nine-year-old son Tim and I began our daily running streak last August, foreseeing what a long, snowy, cold, icy winter we were in for wouldn't have discouraged me from attempting a full year of daily running. Realizing that it was a Leap Year and we'd have to pull off a 366th day in order to complete our year, on the other hand, might have been enough to keep me from ever putting forth the suggestion that I made to Tim in early August of 2007: "Want to see how many days in a row we can run a mile or more?"

The impetus at the time was a compelling voice telling me that I had to find something Tim could throw himself into as enthusiastically as video games and baseball. And it had to be something that brought us together. He was about to turn nine years old and seemed most attracted to pursuits that held barely any interest for me at all: professional sports, books about wizards, and anything that involved animated characters on a screen. When we began, he'd never run more than a brief soccer-game sprint or the distance around the bases for a home run, so I had no reason to think he'd develop a capacity for long-distance running even if he wanted to. Nor did I guess that he'd want to.

But it was the only idea I had at the time to resolve my determination to find something for us to do together, something that would strengthen our eroding mother-son bond. Let's try it, I urged him. He tried it, and didn't want to stop. He may like the sport of running just fine, but it soon became apparent to me that he liked the absurd discipline of daily "streak running" even more. Much as I had been feeling that doing things with Mom was not a priority for him, he fastened on to the idea that this was something the two of us would commit to every day, and he was hooked.

In the winter, we ran after dark because I wasn't home in time to run in daylight. Going into the plan, I imagined that winter weather would pose the biggest challenge, but we adjusted – with many layers of fleece – to cold and even snow; it turned out to be the summer thunderstorms that most often hampered our plans. There were days in July when we sat in the house timing the silences between thunderclaps the way women in labor time the space between contractions, and rushed out of the house to do our bare-minimum mile when the rumbles finally stretched at least ten minutes apart. One morning on Russell Street Tim burst into tears because a bolt of lightning nearby scared him so badly, but we were surrounded by trees and three miles from home so we pushed onward. There were a couple of falls, some twisted ankles, and a bad cold or two on both of our parts, but there was never a day that we couldn't get out at all. Tim wrote about running in his school journal; I learned to record our progress in a blog.

And on August 15th, our tally reached Day 366. Our fellow Carlislean, Ronald Kmiec, who as Massachusetts' premier streak runner held a streak more than 30 years long, joined us for a 1.9-mile run along the Bedford Road footpath and through the Center that day. My sister and brother-in-law designed commemorative T-shirts, and my mother made a celebratory dinner.

For me, the inevitable question at that point was what next. We'd reached a year; the countdown that we'd maintained to track the final 100 days of our year hit zero. But Tim has no intention of stopping. He believes he's in this for life, "or the next 70 years," as he likes to say. I'm quite certain I don't have 70 more years of running ahead, but I told him I'd stick with it as long as I could.

So we continue. Even though Tim has completed three 5-mile races, distance generally doesn't appeal to him, so we average only about 1.5 miles most days. I'd still like to do more, missing the leisurely 45-minute rambles I used to do when I ran alone. But we're doing something together, and we're having fun, and that was the point all along.

And so on we run.

GUEST RUNNERS AND THEIR HOMETOWNS 8/15/08

Ronald K. – Carlisle, MA
Holly W. - Carlisle, MA
Cole H. - Carlisle, MA
Robert R. - Swarthmore, PA
Lauren S. - Swarthmore, PA
Nathan B. - Carlisle, MA
John M. - Washington, DC
John L. - Nashua, NH
Eric M. - Carlisle, MA
Nicole P. - Carlisle, MA
Austin P. - Carlisle, MA

Sophie R. - Swarthmore, PA
Alyssa A. - Sandwich, MA

DOGS
Tillie T. - Carlisle, MA
Angus P. - Carlisle, MA

STUFFED ANIMALS
Ba W. (a frog) - Carlisle, MA
Vicon W. (an elephant) - Carlisle, MA

CHAPTER 13

August 16, 2009

On August 16th, 2009, Tim played baseball and went for a bike ride. But, for the first time in 732 days, he did not run a mile. He had continued our streak for a second full year and then one more day so that he could run on our official streak anniversary day, August 15th. But two months earlier he had begun making noises about ending the streak once we reached two years, and he was ready to stop. Baseball was taking up even more of his time in the summer of 2009 than it had previously, and he was tired of trying to squish in a run before practice or after a late game. It made him realize that the commitment of daily running might be more than he wanted to take on at this time in his life.

I decided not to stop when he did. During our second year of running, we hadn't run together nearly as much as the first year. Tim grew fond of running alone, and often went out without me just to enjoy the solitude. We had gone on separate weeklong vacations early in the summer as well – Tim played in a baseball tournament in Cooperstown, New York, while I attended a writers' conference in Colorado – and by that time it was natural for us to run separately. Though I'm not sure what the point of the streak is for me now that Tim has discontinued, I'm not ready to give up on it quite yet.

Rick succeeded at weight loss – he has lost fifty pounds since having surgery – but gave up on the dream of having his own consulting business and accepted a job as a financial planner for a large company. I'm continuing to work from home on a variety of freelance contracts, including the municipal consulting firm (they haven't fired me yet). Kate rides her horses every day and doesn't talk about her health. Ronald Kmiec is continuing on the streak he began after his heart attack, and ran his thirty-fifth consecutive Boston Marathon in April. Holly grew happier and less tantrum-prone but still has a host of imaginary friends and now runs a pretend store out of her room. We still live on the farm but believe that downsizing is the best option if we can find a buyer. So far we haven't, so we continue to enjoy the livestock, the fields, and having my parents next door.

In the time since our running streak began, a lot of people have asked me what I think Tim learned from the project, and even more people have speculated on what *they* think Tim learned. Very few people – Ronald Kmiec being one of the exceptions – have asked me what *I* learned.

Although the words people tend to use when they conjecture about Tim's lessons include "commitment," "determination," "perseverance," what I actually think the most significant skill that streak running brought to Tim was time management. And I do not say that glibly, since time management has been and continues to be one of the major challenges of my adult life. Tim learned that if you are bound and determined to carve ten minutes out of every day in order to run a mile, you find the time. Sometimes that means setting your alarm ten minutes early, and other times it means dealing with the discomfort of running in pouring rain. It might mean ten minutes less of video games or going out right after dinner to run on a full stomach. He has learned in this way to shape time to his own purposes – to look at the twenty-four hours in a day and figure out how to manipulate them to meet his needs – in a way that I consider to be a very valuable life skill.

What I've learned is harder for me to articulate, in part because it circles back to the fundamental questions with which I began the project: Was it my *right* as a parent to try to change my child? Because let's be honest about this: that's what I was ultimately trying to do. I looked at my seemingly pallid, somewhat sulky child and believed that I could form him into my image of a runner: robust, energetic, cheerful. And even in attempting that, I knew it was questionable that I should be trying to change my child's personality at all, in the same way that some parents question the ethics of giving their hyperactive child medication to calm him down. To what extent do we have the right to change our children's natural tendencies? On the other hand, to what extent can we not, if the possibility exists and we genuinely believe it's for the better?

Regardless, running didn't *change* Tim; it *augmented* him. I thought, irrationally, that he would be converted: that running would inspire him to give up the video games, that pounding down the open road would end his attraction to the couch. But no: instead, it opened a new avenue in his personality. He didn't give up one way of being for the other: he is both.

I loved him the way he was; I love him the way he is now. And perhaps that's been the biggest lesson for me as a parent: we love them no matter what, and we can't really change them. But we also shouldn't pass up the opportunity to help them grow... in all kinds of ways, whenever and wherever we see the possibility.

ACKNOWLEDGMENTS

Friends, relatives, neighbors and colleagues too numerous to name contributed to my growth as a person and as a writer over the time that this project has developed. The influence of every single one of them shines through.

In particular, I'd like to thank Jacquie Flynn, literary agent at Joelle Delbourgo Associates, for her encouragement and expertise; Ronald and Leslie Kmiec for introducing us to the concept of streak running and supporting our efforts with so much enthusiasm; Nicole Pinard, Erin McCormack, Nancy Cowan, Julie Baher and Leah Osterman for their insightful comments on earlier drafts of this book; my parents, Carolyn and Dick Shohet, and my parents-in-law, Joanne and Dick West, for their seemingly infinite stores of love and encouragement; everyone on our "guest list" who ran with us throughout the year; Pat Spitzmiller and Mary Dominick for an amazingly generous gesture that brought me to the Aspen Summer Words conference and helped make this writing project a reality; my sisters, Sarah Shohet and Lauren Shohet, along with their husbands; and finally, my son Tim for saying, "Okay, I'll try that." *(I love you, Tim!)*

Made in the USA
Charleston, SC
19 November 2010